Ben Stacy Jerrik (Ed.)

DEGIMA (Computer Cluster)

Ben Stacy Jerrik (Ed.)

DEGIMA (Computer Cluster)

Nagasaki University, N-body simulation, DDR3 SDRAM

Part Press

Contents

Articles

References

DEGIMA_(computer_cluster)

The **DEGIMA** (**DE**stination for **G**pu **I**ntensive **MA**chine) is a high performance computer cluster used for hierarchical N-body simulations at the Nagasaki Advanced Computing Center, Nagasaki University.

The system consists of a 144-node cluster of PCs connected via an InfiniBand interconnect. Each node is composed of 2.66 GHz Intel Core i7 920 processor, two GeForce GTX295 graphics cards, 12 GB DDR3-1333 memory and Mellanox MHES14-XTC SDR InfiniBand host adaptor on MSI X58 pro-E mother board. Each graphics card has two GT200 GPU chips. As a whole, the system has 144 CPUs and 576 GPUs. It runs astrophysical N-body simulations with over 3,000,000,000 particles using the Multiple-Walk parallel treecode.[1] The system is noted for being highly cost and energy-efficient, having a peak performance of 111 TFLOPS with an energy efficiency of 1376 MFLOPS/watt. The overall cost of the hardware was approximately US$500,000.[2] [3]

The name of the system is also derived from the name of a small artificial island called "Dejima" in Nagasaki.

See also

- Supercomputing in Japan

References

[1] Hamada T. *et al.* (2009) A novel multiple-walk parallel algorithm for the Barnes–Hut treecode on GPUs – towards cost effective, high performance N-body simulation. *Comput. Sci. Res. Development* 24:21-31. doi:10.1007/s00450-009-0089-1

[2] The Green500 June 2011 (http://www.green500.org/lists/2011/06/top/list.php) Environmentally Responsible Supercomputing, The Green500 List

[3] Hamada T., Nitadori K. (2010) 190 TFlops astrophysical N-body simulation on a cluster of GPUs. In *Proceedings of the 2010 ACM/IEEE International Conference for High Performance Computing, Networking, Storage and Analysis* (SC '10). IEEE Computer Society, Washington, DC, USA, 1-9. doi:10.1109/SC.2010.1

Nagasaki_University

<table>
<tr><td colspan="2" align="center">Nagasaki University</td></tr>
<tr><td colspan="2" align="center">(Nagasaki Daigaku)</td></tr>
<tr><td>Established</td><td>1949</td></tr>
<tr><td>Type</td><td>National</td></tr>
<tr><td>President</td><td>Shigeru Katamine</td></tr>
<tr><td>Location</td><td>Nagasaki, Nagasaki Prefecture, Japan</td></tr>
<tr><td>Campus</td><td>Urban</td></tr>
<tr><td>Website</td><td>Nagasaki University [1]</td></tr>
</table>

Nagasaki University (*Nagasaki daigaku*) is a national university of Japan. Its nickname is *Chōdai* (). The main campus is located in Bunkyo-machi, Nagasaki City, Nagasaki Prefecture, Japan.

History

Nagasaki University was established in 1949 by incorporating several national institutions, namely, Nagasaki Medical College (including College Hospital and College of Pharmaceutical Sciences), Nagasaki College of Economics, Nagasaki Normal School, Nagasaki Youth Normal School and Nagasaki High School.[2]

The new main campus (Bunkyo Campus) was formerly a plant site of Mitsubishi Arms Factory (Ohashi Plant).[3]

Nagasaki Medical College in the Meiji Era

Nagasaki Medical College

The oldest of the predecessors was Nagasaki Medical College. It was founded in November 1857 as Medical Training Institute (*Igaku denshūsho*) by the branch office of Tokugawa Shogunate. The first professor was J. L. C. Pompe van Meerdervoort, and the institute was one of the first[4] western-style (not *Kampō*) medical schools in Japan. In 1861 the hospital was founded, and after Meiji Restoration the school became a public (prefectural, later national) medical school. It was developed into Nagasaki Vocational School of Medicine (*Nagasaki igaku senmon gakkō*)[2] in 1901, then into Nagasaki Medical College (*Nagasaki ika daigaku*) in 1923.

After Japan participated in the Pacific War, the medical college added several institutes for the war, such as Temporary College of Medicine (1940) and East Asia Research Institute of Endemics (1942, Institute of Tropical Medicine today). On August 9, 1945 the college was heavily damaged by the atomic bomb, because it

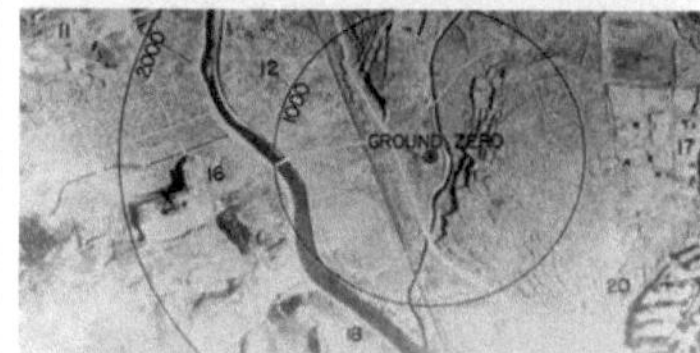
Nagasaki before and after the Atomic Bombing. "17": Nagasaki Medical College, "20": Hospital

was located only 500 to 700 meters away from the hypocenter.[3] Over 800 professors, students and medical workers were killed. The college was moved to Omura in September 1945, and then to Isahaya in 1946. The old campus (Sakamoto Campus) was restored later in 1950, after the college was integrated into Nagasaki University.

Nagasaki College of Economics

Another notable predecessor was Nagasaki College of Economics. It was founded in March 1905 as Nagasaki Higher Commercial School (*Nagasaki kōtō shōgyō gakkō*). It was

Keirin Hall at Katafuchi Campus, built in 1919

the fourth national commercial college in Japan, after Tokyo (1887), Kobe (1902) and Yamaguchi (February 1905), and aimed at educating students so that they could engage in business with China, Korea and Southeast Asia. In 1917 it added the Advanced Course for Trade (one-year course), and the building for the course was built in 1919 (Keirin Hall today).

In 1944 it was renamed Nagasaki College of Economics (*Nagasaki keizai senmon gakkō*). On August 9, 1945 although Nagasaki underwent the atomic bombing, the college buildings were protected by Mt. Kompira. Its campus (Katafuchi Campus) has been used by the Faculty of Economics, Nagasaki University.

Undergratuate schools

Bunkyo Campus

- Faculty of Education
- Faculty of Pharmaceutical Sciences
- Faculty of Engineering
- Faculty of Environmental Studies
- Faculty of Fisheries

Sakamoto Campus

- School of Medicine
- School of Dentistry

Katafuchi Campus

- Faculty of Economics

Graduate schools

- Graduate School of Education (Master's courses only)
- Graduate School of Economics
- Graduate School of Science and Technology
- Graduate School of Biomedical Sciences
- Graduate School of International Health Development (Master's courses only)

Research institutes

- Institute of Tropical Medicine
- Atomic Bomb Disease Institute, Nagasaki University Graduate School of Biomedical Sciences

Notable alumni

- Takashi Nagai, physician specializing in radiology, an A-bomb victim.
- Osamu Shimomura,organic chemist and marine biologist, awarded the Nobel Prize in Chemistry in 2008 for his discovery and development of green fluorescent protein (GFP) with two other American chemists.

References

[1] http://www.nagasaki-u.ac.jp/index_en.html

[2] "Nagasaki University: Organization/Historical Sketch" (http://www.nagasaki-u.ac.jp/guidance/gaiyo/h19/h19-001.pdf). . Retrieved 2009-05-16.

[3] "Nagasaki University: Physical Damages caused by the Nagasaki Atomic Bombing" (http://www-sdc.med.nagasaki-u.ac.jp/n50/disaster/D-map.gif). . Retrieved 2009-05-16.

[4] Tohoku University insists that Sendai han school (Tohoku University today) started the first western medical education in 1822. See http://www.med.tohoku.ac.jp/english/history/index.html

External links

- Nagasaki University (http://www.nagasaki-u.ac.jp/index_en.html)

N-body simulation

An *N*-body simulation is a simulation of a dynamical system of particles, usually under the influence of physical forces, such as gravity (see n-body problem). In cosmology, they are used to study processes of non-linear structure formation such as the process of forming galaxy filaments and galaxy halos from dark matter in physical cosmology. Direct *N*-body simulations are used to study the dynamical evolution of star clusters.

The Millennium Run simulates the universe until the present state, where structures are abundant, manifesting themselves as stars, galaxies and clusters

Nature of the particles

The 'particles' treated by the simulation may or may not correspond to physical objects which are particulate in nature. For example, an N-body simulation of a star cluster might have a particle per star, so each particle has some physical significance. On the other hand a simulation of a gas cloud cannot afford to have a particle for each atom or molecule of gas as this would require billions of particles for each gram of material (see Avogadro constant), so a single 'particle' would represent some much larger quantity of gas. This quantity need not have any physical significance, but must be chosen as a compromise between accuracy and manageable computer requirements.

Direct gravitational *N*-body simulations

In direct gravitational *N*-body simulations, the equations of motion of a system of N particles under the influence of their mutual gravitational forces are integrated numerically without any simplifying approximations. The first direct *N*-body simulations were carried out by Sebastian von Hoerner at the Astronomisches Rechen-Institut in Heidelberg, Germany. Sverre Aarseth at the University of Cambridge (UK) has dedicated his entire scientific life to the development of a series of highly efficient *N*-body codes for astrophysical applications which use adaptive (hierarchical) time steps, an Ahmad-Cohen neighbour scheme and regularization of close encounters. Regularization is a mathematical trick to remove the singularity in the Newtonian law of gravitation for two particles which approach each other arbitrarily close. Sverre Aarseth's codes are used to study the dynamics of star clusters, planetary systems and galactic nuclei.

General relativity simulations

Many simulations are large enough that the effects of general relativity in establishing a Friedmann-Lemaitre-Robertson-Walker cosmology are significant. This is incorporated in the simulation as an evolving measure of distance (or scale factor) in a comoving coordinate system, which causes the particles to slow in comoving coordinates (as well as due to the redshifting of their physical energy). However, the contributions of general relativity and the finite speed of gravity can otherwise be ignored, as typical dynamical timescales are long compared to the light crossing time for the simulation, and the space-time curvature induced by the particles and the particle velocities are small. The boundary conditions of these cosmological simulations are usually periodic (or toroidal), so that one edge of the simulation volume matches up with the opposite edge.

Calculation optimizations

N-body simulations are simple in principle, because they merely involve integrating the $6N$ ordinary differential equations defining the particle motions in Newtonian gravity. In practice, the number N of particles involved is usually very large (typical simulations include many millions, the Millennium simulation includes ten billion) and the number of particle-particle interactions needing to be computed increases as N^2, and so ordinary methods of integrating numerical differential equations, such as the Runge-Kutta method, are inadequate. Therefore, a number of refinements are commonly used.

One of the simplest refinements is that each particle carries with it its own timestep variable, so that particles with widely different dynamical times don't all have to be evolved forward at the rate of that with the shortest time.

There are two basic algorithms by which the simulation may be optimised.

Tree methods

In **tree methods** such as a Barnes–Hut simulation, the volume is usually divided up into cubic cells in an octree, so that only particles from nearby cells need to be treated individually, and particles in distant cells can be treated as a single large particle centered at its center of mass (or as a low-order multipole expansion). This can dramatically reduce the number of particle pair interactions that must be computed. To prevent the simulation from becoming swamped by computing particle-particle interactions, the cells must be refined to smaller cells in denser parts of the simulation which contain many particles per cell. For simulations where particles are not evenly distributed, the well-separated pair decomposition methods of Callahan and Kosaraju yield optimal O(n log n) time per iteration with fixed dimension.

Particle mesh method

Another possibility is the **particle mesh method** in which space is discretised on a mesh and, for the purposes of computing the gravitational potential, particles are assumed to be divided between the nearby vertices of the mesh. Finding the potential energy Φ is easy, because the Poisson equation

where G is Newton's constant and is the density (number of particles at the mesh points), is trivial to solve by using the fast Fourier transform to go to the frequency domain where the Poisson equation has the simple form

where is the comoving wavenumber and the hats denote Fourier transforms. The gravitational field can now be found by multiplying by and computing the inverse Fourier transform (or computing the inverse transform and then using some other method). Since this method is limited by the mesh size, in practice a smaller mesh or some other technique (such as combining with a tree or simple particle-particle algorithm) is used to compute the small-scale forces. Sometimes an adaptive mesh is used, in which the mesh cells are much smaller in the denser regions of the simulation.

Two-particle systems

Although there are millions or billions of particles in typical simulations, they typically correspond to a real particle with a very large mass, typically 10^9 solar masses. This can introduce problems with short-range interactions between the particles such as the formation of two-particle binary systems. As the particles are meant to represent large numbers of dark matter particles or groups of stars, these binaries are unphysical. To prevent this, a softened Newtonian force law is used, which does not diverge as the inverse-square radius at short distances. Most simulations implement this quite naturally by running the simulations on cells of finite size. It is important to implement the discretization procedure in such a way that particles always exert a vanishing force on themselves.

Incorporating baryons, leptons and photons into simulations

Many simulations simulate only cold dark matter, and thus include only the gravitational force. Incorporating baryons, leptons and photons into the simulations dramatically increases their complexity and often radical simplifications of the underlying physics must be made. However, this is an extremely important area and many modern simulations are now trying to understand processes that occur during galaxy formation which could account for galaxy bias.

See also

- Millennium Run
- Structure formation
- Large-scale structure of the cosmos
- GADGET
- Galaxy formation and evolution
- *n*-body problem
- natural units
- Virgo Consortium

References

- Sebastian von Hoerner (1960). "Die numerische Integration des n-Körper-Problemes für Sternhaufen. I". *Zeitschrift für Astrophysik* **50**: 184. Bibcode 1960ZA.....50..184V.
- Sebastian von Hoerner (1963). "Die numerische Integration des *n*-Körper-Problemes für Sternhaufen. II". *Zeitschrift für Astrophysik* **57**: 47. Bibcode 1963ZA.....57...47V.
- Sverre J. Aarseth (2003). *Gravitational* N-*body Simulations: Tools and Algorithms*. Cambridge University Press. ISBN 0521121531.
- Edmund Bertschinger (1998). "Simulations of structure formation in the universe" [1]. *Annual Review of Astronomy and Astrophysics* **36** (1): 599–654. Bibcode 1998ARA&A..36..599B. doi:10.1146/annurev.astro.36.1.599.
- James Binney and Scott Tremaine (1988). *Galactic Dynamics*. Princeton University Press. ISBN ISBN 0-691-08445-9.
- A survey of all known *N*-body simulation methods [2]
- Callahan, Paul B.; Kosaraju, Sambasiva Rao (1992). "A decomposition of multidimensional point sets with applications to *k*-nearest-neighbors and n-body potential fields (preliminary version)". *STOC '92: Proc. ACM Symp. Theory of Computing*. ACM..

External links

- N-body Simulations [3] on Scholarpedia [4]

References

[1] http://arjournals.annualreviews.org/doi/abs/10.1146%2Fannurev.astro.36.1.599
[2] http://www.amara.com/papers/nbody.html
[3] http://www.scholarpedia.org/article/N-body_simulations
[4] http://www.scholarpedia.org

DDR3_SDRAM

In computing, **DDR3 SDRAM**, an abbreviation for **double data rate type three synchronous dynamic random access memory,** is a modern kind of dynamic random access memory (DRAM) with a high bandwidth interface. It is one of several variants of DRAM and associated interface techniques used since the early 1970s. DDR3 SDRAM is neither forward nor backward compatible with any earlier type of random access memory (RAM) due to different signaling voltages, timings, and other factors.

PC3-10600 DDR3 SO-DIMM (204 pins)

DDR3 is a DRAM interface specification. The actual DRAM arrays that store the data are similar to earlier types, with similar performance.

The primary benefit of DDR3 SDRAM over its immediate predecessor, DDR2 SDRAM, is its ability to transfer data at twice the rate (eight times the speed of its internal memory arrays), enabling higher bandwidth or peak data rates. With two transfers per cycle of a quadrupled clock, a 64-bit wide DDR3 module may achieve a transfer rate of up to 64 times the memory clock speed in megabytes per second (MB/s). With data being transferred 64 bits at a time per memory module, DDR3 SDRAM gives a transfer rate of (memory clock rate) × 4 (for bus clock multiplier) × 2 (for data rate) × 64 (number of bits transferred) / 8 (number of bits/byte). Thus with a memory clock frequency of 100 MHz, DDR3 SDRAM gives a maximum transfer rate of 6400 MB/s. In addition, the DDR3 standard permits chip capacities of up to 8 gigabytes.

Overview

Compared to DDR2 memory, DDR3 memory uses 30% less power. This reduction comes from the difference in supply voltages: 1.8V or 2.5V for DDR2, and 1.5V for DDR3. The 1.5 V supply voltage works well with the 90 nanometer fabrication technology used in the original DDR3 chips. Some manufacturers further propose using "dual-gate" transistors to reduce leakage of current.[1]

According to JEDEC[2] , 1.575 volts should be considered the absolute maximum when memory stability is the foremost consideration, such as in servers or other mission-critical devices. In addition, JEDEC states that memory modules must withstand up to 1.975 volts before incurring permanent damage, although they are not required to function correctly at that level.

The main benefit of DDR3 comes from the higher bandwidth made possible by its prefetch buffer, which is 8-burst-deep. In contrast, the prefetch buffer of DDR2 is 4-burst-deep, and the prefetch buffer of DDR is 2-burst-deep.

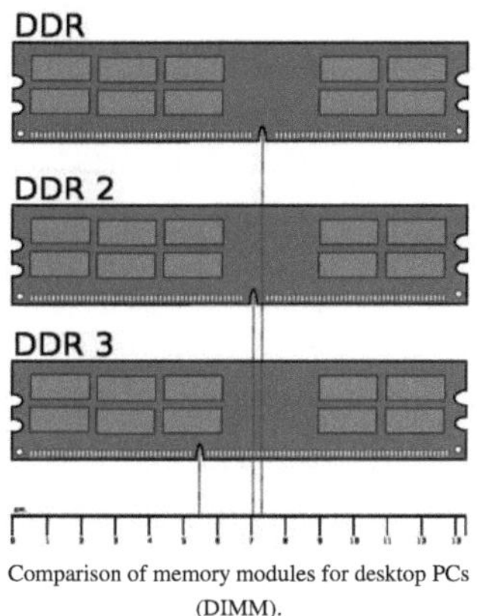

Comparison of memory modules for desktop PCs (DIMM).

DDR3 modules can transfer data at a rate of 800–2133 MT/s using both rising and falling edges of a 400–1066 MHz I/O clock. Sometimes, a vendor may misleadingly advertise the I/O clock rate by labeling the MT/s as MHz. The MT/s is normally twice that of MHz by double sampling, one on the rising clock edge, and the other, on the falling. In comparison, DDR2's current range of data transfer rates is 400–1066 MT/s using a 200–533 MHz I/O clock, and DDR's range is 200–400 MT/s based on a 100–200 MHz I/O clock. High-performance graphics was an initial driver of such bandwidth requirements, where high bandwidth data transfer between framebuffers is required.

DDR3 does use the same electric signaling standard as DDR and DDR2, Stub Series Terminated Logic, albeit at different timings and voltages. Specifically, DDR3 uses SSTL_15.[3]

DDR3 prototypes were announced in early 2005. Products in the form of motherboards appeared on the market in June 2007[4] based on Intel's P35 "Bearlake" chipset with DIMMs at bandwidths up to DDR3-1600 (PC3-12800).[5] The Intel Core i7, released in November 2008, connects directly to memory rather than via a chipset. The Core i7 supports only DDR3. AMD's first socket AM3 Phenom II X4 processors, released in February 2009, were their first to support DDR3.

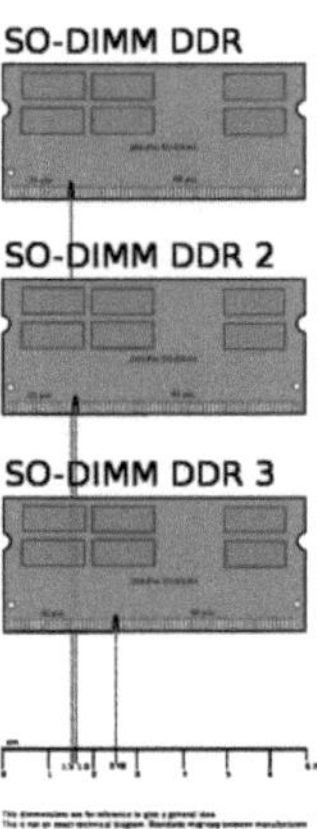

Comparison of memory modules for portable/mobile PCs (SO-DIMM).

DDR3 DIMMs have 240 pins and are electrically incompatible with DDR2. The two are prevented from being accidentally interchanged by different key notch positions on the DIMMs.[6] DDR3 SO-DIMMs have 204 pins.[7]

GDDR3 memory, sometimes incorrectly referred to as "DDR3" due to its similar name, is an entirely different technology, as it is designed for use in graphics cards and is based on DDR2 SDRAM.

DDR3L

The "L" in DDR3L stands for low-voltage. JEDEC introduced two low-voltage standards. The DDR3L standard is 1.35V and has the label "PC3L" for its modules. Examples include DDR3L-800, DDR3L-1066, DDR3L-1333, and DDR3L-1600. The DDR3U standard is 1.25V and has the label "PC3U" for its modules.

Latencies

While the typical latencies for a JEDEC DDR2 device were 5-5-5-15, some standard latencies for JEDEC DDR3 devices include 7-7-7-20 for DDR3-1066 and 8-8-8-24 for DDR3-1333.

DDR3 latencies are numerically higher because the I/O bus clock cycles by which they are measured are shorter; the actual time interval is similar to DDR2 latencies (around 10 ns). There is some improvement because DDR3 generally uses more recent manufacturing processes, but this is not directly caused by the change to DDR3.

As with earlier memory generations, faster DDR3 memory became available after the release of the initial versions. DDR3-2000 memory with 9-9-9-28 latency (9 ns) was available in time to coincide with the Intel Core i7 release.[8] CAS latency of 9 at 1000 MHz (DDR3-2000) is 9 ns, while CAS latency of 7 at 667 MHz (DDR3-1333) is 10.5 ns.

(CAS / Frequency (MHz)) × 1000 = X ns

Example:

(7 / 667) × 1000 = 10.4948 ns

Extensions

Intel Corporation officially introduced the eXtreme Memory Profile (XMP) Specification on March 23, 2007 to enable enthusiast performance extensions to the traditional JEDEC SPD specifications for DDR3 SDRAM.[9]

Modules

JEDEC standard modules

Standard name	Memory clock (MHz)	Cycle time (ns)	I/O bus clock (MHz)	Data rate (MT/s)	Module name	Peak transfer rate (MB/s)	Timings (CL-tRCD-tRP)	CAS latency (ns)
DDR3-800D DDR3-800E	100	10	400	800	PC3-6400	6400	5-5-5 6-6-6	$12\tfrac{1}{2}$ 15
DDR3-1066E DDR3-1066F DDR3-1066G	$133\tfrac{1}{3}$	$7\tfrac{1}{2}$	$533\tfrac{1}{3}$	$1066\tfrac{2}{3}$	PC3-8500	$8533\tfrac{1}{3}$	6-6-6 7-7-7 8-8-8	$11\tfrac{1}{4}$ $13\tfrac{1}{8}$ 15
DDR3-1333F* DDR3-1333G DDR3-1333H DDR3-1333J*	$166\tfrac{2}{3}$	6	$666\tfrac{2}{3}$	$1333\tfrac{1}{3}$	PC3-10600	$10666\tfrac{2}{3}$	7-7-7 8-8-8 9-9-9 10-10-10	$10\tfrac{1}{2}$ 12 $13\tfrac{1}{2}$ 15
DDR3-1600G* DDR3-1600H DDR3-1600J DDR3-1600K	200	5	800	1600	PC3-12800	12800	8-8-8 9-9-9 10-10-10 11-11-11	10 $11\tfrac{1}{4}$ $12\tfrac{1}{2}$ $13\tfrac{3}{4}$
DDR3-1866J* DDR3-1866K DDR3-1866L DDR3-1866M*	$233\tfrac{1}{3}$	$4\tfrac{2}{7}$	$933\tfrac{1}{3}$	$1866\tfrac{2}{3}$	PC3-14900	$14933\tfrac{1}{3}$	10-10-10 11-11-11 12-12-12 13-13-13	$10\tfrac{5}{7}$ $11\tfrac{11}{14}$ $12\tfrac{6}{7}$ $13\tfrac{13}{14}$
DDR3-2133K* DDR3-2133L DDR3-2133M DDR3-2133N*	$266\tfrac{2}{3}$	$3\tfrac{3}{4}$	$1066\tfrac{2}{3}$	$2133\tfrac{1}{3}$	PC3-17000	$17066\tfrac{2}{3}$	11-11-11 12-12-12 13-13-13 14-14-14	$10\tfrac{5}{16}$ $11\tfrac{1}{4}$ $12\tfrac{3}{16}$ $13\tfrac{1}{8}$

* optional

CL - Clock cycles between sending a column address to the memory and the beginning of the data in response

tRCD - Clock cycles between row activate and reads/writes

tRP - Clock cycles between row precharge and activate

Fractional frequencies are normally rounded down, but rounding up to -667 is common due to the exact number being -666⅔ and rounding to the nearest whole number. Some manufacturers also round to a certain precision or round up instead. For example, PC3-10666 memory could be listed as PC3-10600 or PC3-10700.[10]

Note: All items listed above are specified by JEDEC as JESD79-3D.[11] All RAM data rates in-between or above these listed specifications are not standardized by JEDEC—often they are simply manufacturer optimizations using higher-tolerance or overvolted chips. Of these non-standard specifications, the highest reported speed reached was equivalent to DDR3-2544, as of May 2010.[12]

DDR3-xxx denotes data transfer rate, and describes raw DDR chips, whereas PC3-xxxx denotes theoretical bandwidth (with the last two digits truncated), and is used to describe assembled DIMMs. Bandwidth is calculated by taking transfers per second and multiplying by eight. This is because DDR3 memory modules transfer data on a bus that is 64 data bits wide, and since a byte comprises 8 bits, this equates to 8 bytes of data per transfer.

In addition to bandwidth and capacity variants, modules can

1. Optionally implement ECC, which is an extra data byte lane used for correcting minor errors and detecting major errors for better reliability. Modules with ECC are identified by an additional **ECC** or **E** in their designation. For example: "PC3-6400 ECC", or PC3-8500E.[13]

2. Be "registered", which improves signal integrity (and hence potentially clock rates and physical slot capacity) by electrically buffering the signals with a register, at a cost of an extra clock of increased latency. Those modules are identified by an additional **R** in their designation, whereas non-registered (a.k.a. "unbuffered") RAM *may be* identified by an additional **U** in the designation. PC3-6400R is a registered PC3-6400 module, and PC3-6400R ECC is the same module with ECC.

3. Be fully buffered modules, which are designated by **F** or **FB** and do not have the same notch position as other classes. Fully buffered modules cannot be used with motherboards that are made for registered modules, and the different notch position physically prevents their insertion.

Feature summary

DDR3 SDRAM components

- Introduction of asynchronous RESET pin
- Support of system-level flight-time compensation
- On-DIMM mirror-friendly DRAM pinout
- Introduction of CWL (CAS write latency) per clock bin
- On-die I/O calibration engine
- READ and WRITE calibration

DDR3 modules

- Fly-by command/address/control bus with on-DIMM termination
- High-precision calibration resistors
- Are **not** backwards compatible—DDR3 modules do not fit into DDR2 sockets; forcing them can damage the DIMM and/or the motherboard[14]

Technological advantages compared to DDR2

- Higher bandwidth performance, up to 2133 MT/s standardized
- Slightly improved latencies, as measured in nanoseconds
- Higher performance at low power (longer battery life in laptops)
- Enhanced low-power features

Development and market penetration

In May 2005, Desi Rhoden, chairman of the JEDEC committee responsible for creating the DDR3 standard, stated that DDR3 had been under development for "about 3 years".[15] DDR3 was launched in 2007, but sales were not expected to overtake DDR2 until the end of 2009, or possibly early 2010, according to Intel strategist Carlos Weissenberg, speaking during the early part of their roll-out in August 2008.[16] (The same timescale for market penetration had been stated by market intelligence company DRAMeXchange over a year earlier in April 2007,[17] and by Desi Rhoden in 2005.[15]) The primary driving force behind the increased usage of DDR3 has been new Core i7 processors from Intel and Phenom II processors from AMD, both of which have internal memory controllers: the latter recommends DDR3, the former requires it. IDC stated in January 2009 that DDR3 sales will account for 29 percent of the total DRAM units sold in 2009, rising to 72% by 2011.[18]

Successor

JEDEC's planned successor to DDR3 is DDR4, whose standard is currently in development.[19] The primary benefits of DDR4 compared to DDR3 include a higher range of clock frequencies and data transfer rates[20] and significantly lower voltage. Some manufacturers have already demonstrated DDR4 chips for testing purposes.[21]

See also

- Multi-channel memory architecture
- List of device bandwidths

References

[1] McCloskey, Alan, *Research: DDR FAQ* (http://www.ocmodshop.com/ocmodshop.aspx?a=868), , retrieved 2007-10-18

[2] JEDEC JESD 79-3B (http://www.jedec.org/download/search/JESD79-3B.pdf) (section 6, table 21 and section 7, table 23)

[3] Jaci Chang *Design Considerations for the DDR3 Memory Sub-system*. Jedex, 2004, p. 4. http://www.jedex.org/images/pdf/samsung%20-%20jaci_chang.pdf

[4] Soderstrom, Thomas (2007-06-05). "Pipe Dreams: Six P35-DDR3 Motherboards Compared" (http://www.tomshardware.com/2007/06/05/pipe_dreams_six_p35-ddr3_motherboards_compared/). Tom's Hardware. .

[5] Fink, Wesley (2007-07-20). "Super Talent & TEAM: DDR3-1600 Is Here!" (http://www.anandtech.com/printarticle.aspx?i=3045). AnandTech. .

[6] "DocMemory" (2007-02-21). "Memory Module Picture 2007" (http://www.simmtester.com/page/news/showpubnews.asp?title=Memory+Module+Picture+2007&num=150). .

[7] "JEDEC" (2010-12-01). "204-Pin DDR3 SDRAM SO-DIMM Specification" (http://www.jedec.org/download/search/4_20_18R20A.pdf). .

[8] Shilov, Anton (2008-10-29). "Kingston Rolls Out Industry's First 2GHz Memory Modules for Intel Core i7 Platforms" (http://www.xbitlabs.com/news/memory/display/20081029141143_Kingston_Rolls_Out_Industry_s_First_2GHz_Memory_Modules_for_Intel_Core_i7_Platforms.html). Xbit Laboratories. . Retrieved 2008-11-02.

[9] "Intel Extreme memory Profile (Intel XMP) DDR3 Technology" (http://www.intel.com/assets/pdf/whitepaper/319124.pdf). . Retrieved 2009-05-29.

[10] *Pc3 10600 vs. pc3 10666 What's the difference - New-System-Build* (http://www.tomshardware.com/forum/274587-31-10600-10666-what-difference#t2045244), Tomshardware.com, , retrieved 2012-01-23

[11] *DDR3 SDRAM STANDARD* (http://www.jedec.org/standards-documents/docs/jesd-79-3d), Jedec.org, , retrieved 2012-01-23

[12] *Kingston's 2,544 MHz DDR3 On Show at Computex* (http://news.softpedia.com/news/Kingston-s-2-544-MHz-DDR3-On-Show-at-Computex-143379.shtml), News.softpedia.com, 2010-05-31, , retrieved 2012-01-23

[13] *Memory technology evolution: an overview of system memory technologies* (http://h20000.www2.hp.com/bc/docs/support/SupportManual/c00256987/c00256987.pdf) (PDF), Hewlett-Packard, p. 18,

[14] "DDR3: Frequently Asked Questions" (http://www.kingston.com/channelmarketingcenter/hyperx/literature/MKF_1223_DDR3_FAQ.pdf). . Retrieved 2009-08-18.

[15] Sobolev, Vyacheslav (2005-05-31). "JEDEC: Memory standards on the way" (http://www.digitimes.com/news/a20050530PR201.html). digitimes.com. . Retrieved 2011-04-28. *"JEDEC is already well along in the development of the DDR3 standard, and we have been working on it for about three years now.... Following historical models, you could reasonably expect the same three-year transition to a new technology that you have seen for the last several generations of standard memory"*

[16] "IDF: "DDR3 won't catch up with DDR2 during 2009"" (http://www.pcpro.co.uk/news/220257/idf-ddr3-wont-catch-up-with-ddr2-during-2009.html). pcpro.co.uk. 19 August 2008. . Retrieved 2009-06-17.

[17] Bryan, Gardiner (April 17, 2007). "DDR3 Memory Won't Be Mainstream Until 2009" (http://www.extremetech.com/article2/0,2845,2115031,00.asp). extremetech.com. . Retrieved 2009-06-17.

[18] Salisbury, Andy (2009-01-20). "New 50nm Process Will Make DDR3 Faster and Cheaper This Year" (http://www.maximumpc.com/article/news/new_50nm_process_will_make_ddr3_faster_and_cheaper_this_year). maximumpc.com. . Retrieved 2009-06-17.

[19] "KH Kim Receives 2011 JEDEC Technical Recognition Award" (http://www.jedec.org/news/jedec-awards-program/kh-kim-2011-tr-award). jedec.org. . Retrieved 2011-07-31.

[20] Shilov, Anton (August 16, 2010). "Next-Generation DDR4 Memory to Reach 4.266GHz − Report" (http://www.xbitlabs.com/news/memory/display/20100816124343_Next_Generation_DDR4_Memory_to_Reach_4_266GHz_Report.html). Xbitlabs.com. . Retrieved 2011-01-03.

[21] "Samsung develops DDR4 memory with up to 40 percent better energy efficiency than DDR3" (http://www.engadget.com/2011/01/04/samsung-develops-ddr4-memory-with-up-to-40-percent-better-energy/). Engadget.com. January 4, 2011. . Retrieved 2011-07-31.

GeForce_200_Series

	GeForce 200 Series
	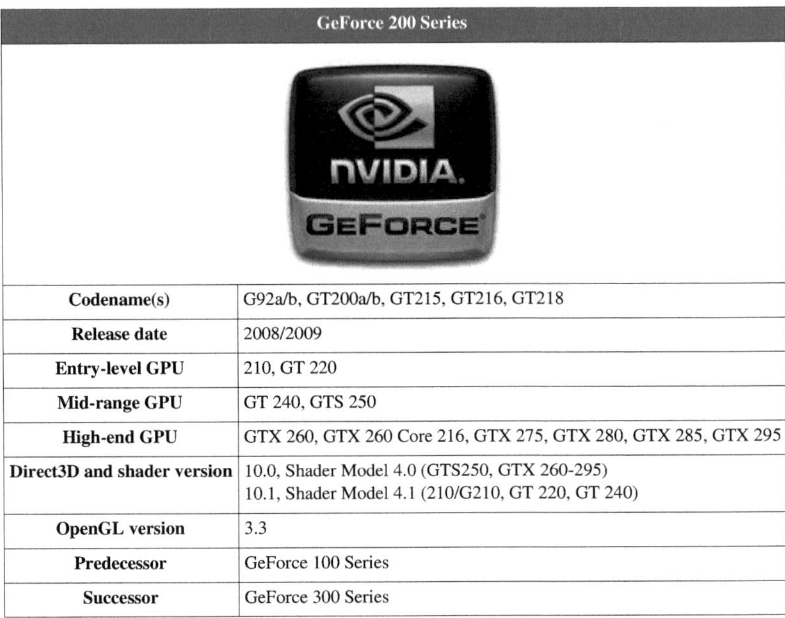
Codename(s)	G92a/b, GT200a/b, GT215, GT216, GT218
Release date	2008/2009
Entry-level GPU	210, GT 220
Mid-range GPU	GT 240, GTS 250
High-end GPU	GTX 260, GTX 260 Core 216, GTX 275, GTX 280, GTX 285, GTX 295
Direct3D and shader version	10.0, Shader Model 4.0 (GTS250, GTX 260-295) 10.1, Shader Model 4.1 (210/G210, GT 220, GT 240)
OpenGL version	3.3
Predecessor	GeForce 100 Series
Successor	GeForce 300 Series

The **GeForce 200 Series** is the 10th generation of Nvidia's GeForce graphics processing units.

Overview

The Geforce 200 Series introduces NVidia's second generation unified shader architecture, the first major update to the company's original unified shader architecture used in the GeForce 8 Series.

The GeForce GTX 280 and GTX 260 are based on the same processor core. During the manufacturing process, GTX chips are binned and separated through defect testing of the core's logic functionality. Those that fail to meet the GTX 280 hardware specification are re-tested and binned as GTX 260 (which is specified with fewer stream processors, less ROPs and a narrower memory bus). Its primary competition came from ATI's Radeon HD 4000 series.

In late 2008, in order to create more parity between the GTX 260 and the competing HD 4870, Nvidia re-released the GTX 260 with 216 stream processors, up from 192. Effectively, there are two GTX 260 cards in production with non-trivial performance differences.

The GeForce 200 series GPUs (GT200a/b GPU), excluding GeForce GTS 250, GTS 240 GPUs (these are older G92b GPUs), have double precision support for use in GPGPU applications. GT200 GPUs also have improved performance in geometry shading.

As of June 2008, the GT200 is the largest commercial GPU ever constructed. It consists of 1.4 billion transistors covering a 576 mm^2 die surface area built on a 65 nm process. To date, the GT200 is the largest CMOS-logic chip that has been fabricated at the TSMC foundry. The GeForce 400 Series have since superseded the GT200 chips in transistor count, but the original GT200 dies still exceed the GF100 die size.

Nvidia officially announced and released the retail version of the previously OEM only GeForce 210 (GT218 GPU) and GeForce GT 220 (GT216 GPU) on October 12, 2009. Nvidia officially announced and released the GeForce GT 240 (GT215 GPU) on November 17, 2009. The new 40nm GPUs feature the new PureVideo HD VP4 decoder hardware in them, the older GeForce 8 and 9 GPUs only have PureVideo HD VP2 or VP3(G98). They also support Compute Capability 1.2, whereas older GeForce 8 and 9 GPUs only supported Compute Capability 1.1. All GT21x GPUs also contain an audio processor inside and support 8 channel LPCM output through HDMI.

See also

- Comparison of Nvidia graphics processing units
- GeForce 8 Series
- GeForce 9 Series
- GeForce 400 Series
- GeForce 500 Series
- GeForce 600 Series
- Nvidia Quadro - Nvidia's workstation graphics solution
- Nvidia Tesla - Nvidia's first dedicated general purpose GPU (graphical processor unit)

References

External links

- GeForce GTX 295 (http://www.nvidia.com/object/product_geforce_gtx_295_us.html)
- GeForce GTX 285 (http://www.nvidia.com/object/product_geforce_gtx_285_us.html)
- GeForce GTX 280 (http://www.nvidia.com/object/product_geforce_gtx_280_us.html)
- GeForce GTX 275 (http://www.nvidia.com/object/product_geforce_gtx_275_us.html)
- GeForce GTX 260 (http://www.nvidia.com/object/product_geforce_gtx_260_us.html)
- GeForce GTS 250 (http://www.nvidia.com/object/product_geforce_gts_250_us.html)
- GeForce GTS 240 (OEM) (http://www.nvidia.com/object/product_geforce_gts_240_us.html)
- GeForce GT 240 (http://www.nvidia.com/object/product_geforce_gt_240_us.html)
- GeForce GT 220 (http://www.nvidia.com/object/product_geforce_gt_220_us.html)
- GeForce 210 (http://www.nvidia.com/object/product_geforce_210_us.html)
- GeForce 205 (http://www.nvidia.com/object/product_geforce_205_us.html)
- GeForce GTX 285M (http://www.nvidia.com/object/product_geforce_gtx_285m_us.html)
- GeForce GTX 280M (http://www.nvidia.com/object/product_geforce_gtx_280m_us.html)
- GeForce GTX 260M (http://www.nvidia.com/object/product_geforce_gtx_260m_us.html)
- GeForce GTS 260M (http://www.nvidia.com/object/product_geforce_gts_260m_us.html)
- GeForce GTS 250M (http://www.nvidia.com/object/product_geforce_gts_250m_us.html)
- GeForce GT 240M (http://www.nvidia.com/object/product_geforce_gt_240m_us.html)
- GeForce GT 230M (http://www.nvidia.com/object/product_geforce_gt_230m_us.html)
- GeForce G210M (http://www.nvidia.com/object/product_geforce_g210m_us.html)
- Nvidia Parallel Nsight (http://developer.nvidia.com/nvidia-parallel-nsight)

Graphics_processing_unit

A **graphics processing unit** or **GPU** (also occasionally called **visual processing unit** or **VPU**) is a specialized electronic circuit designed to rapidly manipulate and alter memory in such a way so as to accelerate the building of images in a frame buffer intended for output to a display. GPUs are used in embedded systems, mobile phones, personal computers, workstations, and game consoles. Modern GPUs are very efficient at manipulating computer graphics, and their highly parallel structure makes them more effective than general-purpose CPUs for algorithms where processing of large blocks of data is done in parallel. In a personal computer, a GPU can be present on a video card, or it can be on the motherboard or—in certain CPUs—on the CPU die. More than 90% of new desktop and notebook computers have integrated GPUs, which are usually far less powerful than those on a dedicated video card.[1]

GeForce 6600GT (NV43) GPU

The term was popularized by Nvidia in 1999, who marketed the GeForce 256 as "the world's first 'GPU', or Graphics Processing Unit, a single-chip processor with integrated transform, lighting, triangle setup/clipping, and rendering engines that is capable of processing a minimum of 10 million polygons per second". Rival ATI Technologies coined the term visual processing unit or VPU with the release of the Radeon 9700 in 2002.

History

1980s

In 1983 Intel made the iSBX 275 Video Graphics Controller Multimodule Board for industrial systems based on the Multibus standard.[2] The card was based on the 82720 Graphics Display Controller and accelerated the drawing of lines, arcs, rectangles, and character bitmaps. The framebuffer was also accelerated through loading via DMA. The board was intended for use with Intel's line of Multibus industrial single board computer plugin cards.

In 1986, Texas Instruments released the TMS34010, the first microprocessor with on-chip graphics capabilities. It could run general-purpose code, but it had a very graphics-oriented instruction set. In 1990-1991, this chip became the basis of the Texas Instruments Graphics Architecture ("TIGA") Windows accelerator cards.

In 1987, the IBM 8514 graphics system was released as one of the first video cards for IBM PC compatibles to implement fixed-function 2D primitives in electronic hardware.

1990s

In 1991, S3 Graphics introduced the *S3 86C911*, which its designers named after the Porsche 911 as an indication of the performance increase it promised. The 86C911 spawned a host of imitators: by 1995, all major PC graphics chip makers had added 2D acceleration support to their chips. By this time, fixed-function *Windows accelerators* had surpassed expensive general-purpose graphics coprocessors in Windows performance, and these coprocessors faded away from the PC market.

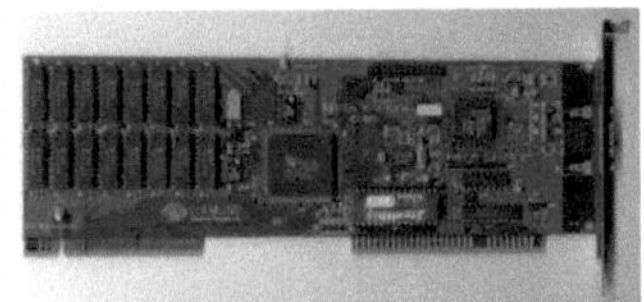

Tseng Labs ET4000/W32p

Throughout the 1990s, 2D GUI acceleration continued to evolve. As manufacturing capabilities improved, so did the level of integration of graphics chips. Additional application programming interfaces (APIs) arrived for a variety of tasks, such as Microsoft's WinG graphics library for Windows 3.x, and their later DirectDraw interface for hardware acceleration of 2D games within Windows 95 and later.

In the early and mid-1990s, CPU-assisted real-time 3D graphics were becoming increasingly common in computer and console games, which led to an increasing public demand for hardware-accelerated 3D graphics. Early examples of mass-marketed 3D graphics hardware can be found in fifth generation video game consoles such as PlayStation and Nintendo 64. In the PC world, notable failed first-tries for low-cost 3D graphics chips were the S3 *ViRGE*, ATI *Rage*, and Matrox *Mystique*. These chips were essentially previous-generation 2D accelerators with 3D features bolted on. Many were even pin-compatible with the earlier-generation chips for ease of implementation and minimal cost. Initially, performance 3D graphics were possible only with discrete boards dedicated to accelerating 3D functions (and lacking 2D GUI acceleration entirely) such as the 3dfx *Voodoo*. However, as manufacturing technology again progressed, video, 2D GUI acceleration, and 3D functionality were all integrated into one chip. Rendition's *Verite* chipsets were the first to do this well enough to be worthy of note.

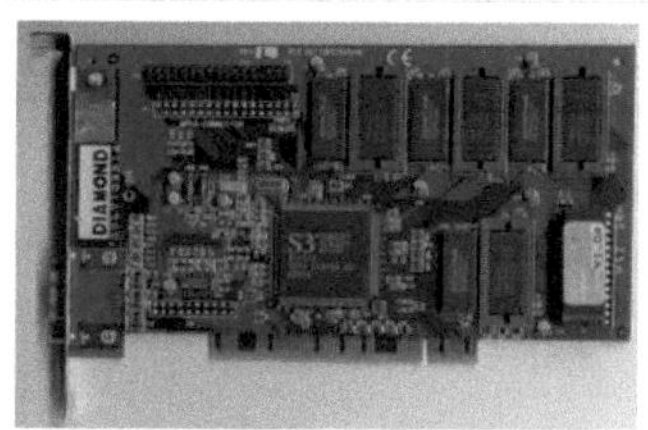

S3 Graphics ViRGE

Voodoo3 2000 AGP card

OpenGL appeared in the early 90s as a professional graphics API, but originally suffered from performance issues which allowed the Glide API to step in and become a dominant force on the PC in the late 90s.[3] However these issues were quickly overcome and the Glide API fell by the wayside. Software implementations of OpenGL were common during this time although the influence of OpenGL eventually led to widespread hardware support. Over time a parity emerged between features offered in hardware and those offered in OpenGL. DirectX became popular among Windows game developers during the late 90s. Unlike OpenGL, Microsoft insisted on providing strict one-to-one support of hardware. The approach made DirectX less popular as a stand alone graphics API initially since many GPUs provided their own specific features, which existing OpenGL applications were already able to benefit from, leaving DirectX often one generation behind. (See: Comparison of OpenGL and Direct3D).

Over time Microsoft began to work more closely with hardware developers, and started to target the releases of DirectX with those of the supporting graphics hardware. Direct3D 5.0 was the first version of the burgeoning API to gain widespread adoption in the gaming market, and it competed directly with many more hardware specific, often proprietary graphics libraries, while OpenGL maintained a strong following. Direct3D 7.0 introduced support for hardware-accelerated transform and lighting (T&L) for Direct3D, while OpenGL already had this capability already exposed from its inception. 3D accelerators moved beyond being just simple rasterizers to add another significant hardware stage to the 3D rendering pipeline. The Nvidia *GeForce 256* (also known as NV10) was the first consumer-level card on the market with hardware-accelerated T&L, while professional 3D cards already had this capability. Hardware transform and lighting, both already existing features of OpenGL, came to consumer-level hardware in the 90s and set the precedent for later pixel shader and vertex shader units which were far more flexible and programmable.

2000 to present

With the advent of the OpenGL API and similar functionality in DirectX, GPUs added programmable shading to their capabilities. Each pixel could now be processed by a short program that could include additional image textures as inputs, and each geometric vertex could likewise be processed by a short program before it was projected onto the screen. Nvidia was first to produce a chip capable of programmable shading, the *GeForce 3* (code named NV20). By October 2002, with the introduction of the ATI *Radeon 9700* (also known as R300), the world's first Direct3D 9.0 accelerator, pixel and vertex shaders could implement looping and lengthy floating point math, and in general were quickly becoming as flexible as CPUs, and orders of magnitude faster for image-array operations. Pixel shading is often used for things like bump mapping, which adds texture, to make an object look shiny, dull, rough, or even round or extruded.[4]

As the processing power of GPUs has increased, so has their demand for electrical power. High performance GPUs often consume more energy than current CPUs.[5] See also performance per watt and quiet PC.

Today, parallel GPUs have begun making computational inroads against the CPU, and a subfield of research, dubbed GPU Computing or GPGPU for *General Purpose Computing on GPU*, has found its way into fields as diverse as machine learning,[6] oil exploration, scientific image processing, linear algebra,[7] statistics,[8] 3D reconstruction and even stock options pricing determination. Nvidia's CUDA platform was the earliest widely adopted programming model for GPU computing. More recently OpenCL has become broadly supported. OpenCL is an open standard defined by the Khronos Group.[9] OpenCL solutions are supported by Intel, AMD, Nvidia, and ARM, and according to a recent report by Evan's data Open CL is the GPGPU development platform most widely used by developers in both the US and Asia Pacific.

GPU companies

Many companies have produced GPUs under a number of brand names. In 2008, Intel, Nvidia and AMD/ATI were the market share leaders, with 49.4%, 27.8% and 20.6% market share respectively. However, those numbers include Intel's integrated graphics solutions as GPUs. Not counting those numbers, Nvidia and ATI control nearly 100% of the market.[10] In addition, S3 Graphics,[11] VIA Technologies [12] and Matrox [13] produce GPUs.

Computational functions

Modern GPUs use most of their transistors to do calculations related to 3D computer graphics. They were initially used to accelerate the memory-intensive work of texture mapping and rendering polygons, later adding units to accelerate geometric calculations such as the rotation and translation of vertices into different coordinate systems. Recent developments in GPUs include support for programmable shaders which can manipulate vertices and textures with many of the same operations supported by CPUs, oversampling and interpolation techniques to reduce aliasing, and very high-precision color spaces. Because most of these computations involve matrix and vector operations, engineers and scientists have increasingly studied the use of GPUs for non-graphical calculations. An example of GPUs being used non-graphically is the generation of Bitcoins, where the graphical processing unit is used to solve puzzles.

In addition to the 3D hardware, today's GPUs include basic 2D acceleration and framebuffer capabilities (usually with a VGA compatibility mode).

GPU accelerated video decoding

Most GPUs made since 1995 support the YUV color space and hardware overlays, important for digital video playback, and many GPUs made since 2000 also support MPEG primitives such as motion compensation and iDCT. This process of hardware accelerated video decoding, where portions of the video decoding process and video post-processing are offloaded to the GPU hardware, is commonly referred to as *"GPU accelerated video decoding"*, *"GPU assisted video decoding"*, *"GPU hardware accelerated video decoding"* or *"GPU hardware assisted video decoding"*.

More recent graphics cards even decode high-definition video on the card, offloading the central processing unit. The most common APIs for GPU accelerated video decoding are DxVA for Microsoft Windows

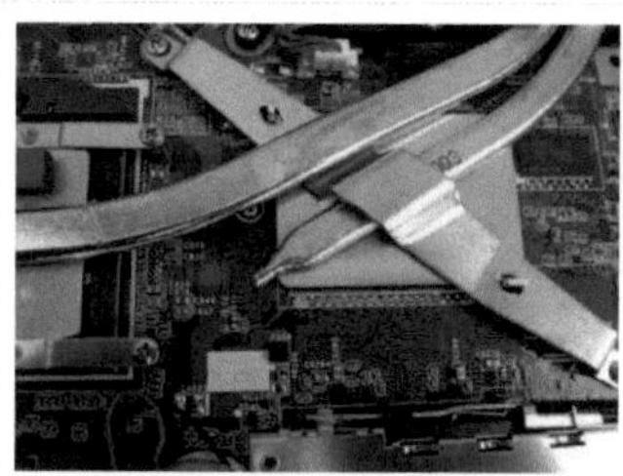

The ATI HD5470 GPU (above) features UVD 2.1 which enables it to decode AVC and VC-1 video formats- GPU from Vaio E series laptop

operating system, VDPAU, VAAPI, XvMC, and XvBA for Linux and UNIX based operating-system. All except XvMC are capable of decoding videos encoded with MPEG-1, MPEG-2, MPEG-4 ASP (MPEG-4 Part 2), MPEG-4 AVC (H.264 / DivX 6), VC-1, WMV3/WMV9, Xvid / OpenDivX (DivX 4), and DivX 5 codecs, while XvMC is only capable of decoding MPEG-1 and MPEG-2.

Video decoding processes that can be accelerated

The video decoding processes that can be accelerated by today's modern GPU hardware are:

- Motion compensation (mocomp)
- Inverse discrete cosine transform (iDCT)
  - Inverse telecine 3:2 and 2:2 pull-down correction
- Inverse modified discrete cosine transform (iMDCT)
- In-loop deblocking filter
- Intra-frame prediction
- Inverse quantization (IQ)
- Variable-Length Decoding (VLD), more commonly known as slice-level acceleration
- Spatial-temporal deinterlacing and automatic interlace/progressive source detection
- Bitstream processing (CAVLC/CABAC).And perfect pixels positioning.

GPU forms

Dedicated graphics cards

The GPUs of the most powerful class typically interface with the motherboard by means of an expansion slot such as PCI Express (PCIe) or Accelerated Graphics Port (AGP) and can usually be replaced or upgraded with relative ease, assuming the motherboard is capable of supporting the upgrade. A few graphics cards still use Peripheral Component Interconnect (PCI) slots, but their bandwidth is so limited that they are generally used only when a PCIe or AGP slot is not available.

A dedicated GPU is not necessarily removable, nor does it necessarily interface with the motherboard in a standard fashion. The term "dedicated" refers to the fact that dedicated graphics cards have RAM that is dedicated to the card's use, not to the fact that *most* dedicated GPUs are removable. Dedicated GPUs for portable computers are most commonly interfaced through a non-standard and often proprietary slot due to size and weight constraints. Such ports may still be considered PCIe or AGP in terms of their logical host interface, even if they are not physically interchangeable with their counterparts.

Technologies such as SLI by Nvidia and CrossFire by ATI allow multiple GPUs to be used to draw a single image, increasing the processing power available for graphics.

Integrated graphics solutions

Integrated graphics solutions, **shared graphics solutions**, or **Integrated graphics processors (IGP)** utilize a portion of a computer's system RAM rather than dedicated graphics memory. They are integrated into the motherboard. Exceptions are AMD's IGPs that use dedicated sideport memory on certain motherboards, and APUs, where they are integrated with the CPU die. Computers with integrated graphics account for 90% of all PC shipments.[14] These solutions are less costly to implement than dedicated graphics solutions, but tend to be less capable. Historically, integrated solutions were often considered unfit to play 3D games or run graphically intensive programs but could run less intensive programs such as Adobe Flash. Examples of such IGPs would be offerings from SiS and VIA circa 2004.[15] However, modern integrated graphics processors such as AMD's Fusion IGPs and Intel's HD Graphics are more than capable of handling 2D graphics from Adobe Flash or low stress 3D graphics, but struggle with the latest games like Battlefield 3. IGPs like the Intel's HD Graphics 3000 and AMD's Fusion IGPs have improved performance that may match cheap dedicated graphic cards, but still lag behind the more expensive dedicated graphics cards. While older platforms had the IGP integrated onto the motherboard, newer platforms (Intel Core i series and AMD Fusion) integrate the GPU right onto the CPU die.

As a GPU is extremely memory intensive, an integrated solution may find itself competing for the already relatively slow system RAM with the CPU, as it has minimal or no dedicated video memory. IGPs can have up to 29.856 GB/s of memory bandwidth from system RAM, however graphics cards can enjoy up to 264GB/sec of bandwidth over PCIe 3.0. Older integrated graphics chipsets lacked hardware transform and lighting, but newer ones include it.[16] [17]

Hybrid solutions

This newer class of GPUs competes with integrated graphics in the low-end desktop and notebook markets. The most common implementations of this are ATI's HyperMemory and Nvidia's TurboCache. Hybrid graphics cards are somewhat more expensive than integrated graphics, but much less expensive than dedicated graphics cards. These share memory with the system and have a small dedicated memory cache, to make up for the high latency of the system RAM. Technologies within PCI Express can make this possible. While these solutions are sometimes advertised as having as much as 768MB of RAM, this refers to how much can be shared with the system memory.

Stream Processing and General Purpose GPUs (GPGPU)

It is becoming increasing common to use a general purpose graphics processing unit as a modified form of stream processor. This concept turns the massive floating-point computational power of a modern graphics accelerator's shader pipeline into general-purpose computing power, as opposed to being hard wired solely to do graphical operations. In certain applications requiring massive vector operations, this can yield several orders of magnitude higher performance than a conventional CPU. The two largest discrete (see "Dedicated graphics cards" above) GPU designers, ATI and Nvidia, are beginning to pursue this new approach with an array of applications. Both Nvidia and ATI have teamed with Stanford University to create a GPU-based client for the Folding@home distributed computing project, for protein folding calculations. In certain circumstances the GPU calculates forty times faster than the conventional CPUs traditionally used by such applications.[18] [19]

GPGPU can be used for many types of embarrassingly parallel task including ray tracing, computational fluid dynamics and weather modelling. They are generally suited to high-throughput type computations that exhibit data-parallelism to exploit the wide vector width SIMD architecture of the GPU.

Furthermore, GPU-based high performance computers are starting to play a significant role in large-scale modelling. Three of the 5 most powerful supercomputers in the world take advantage of GPU acceleration. This includes the current leader as of October 2010, Tianhe-1A, which uses the Nvidia Tesla platform.[20]

NVIDIA cards support API extensions to the C programming language such as CUDA ("Compute Unified Device Architecture") and OpenCL. CUDA is specifically for NVIDIA GPUs whilst OpenCL is designed to work across a multitude of architectures including GPU, CPU and DSP (using vendor specific SDKs). These technologies allow specified functions (kernels) from a normal C program to run on the GPU's stream processors. This makes C programs capable of taking advantage of a GPU's ability to operate on large matrices in parallel, while still making use of the CPU when appropriate. CUDA is also the first API to allow CPU-based applications to access directly the resources of a GPU for more general purpose computing without the limitations of using a graphics API.

Since 2005 there has been interest in using the performance offered by GPUs for evolutionary computation in general, and for accelerating the fitness evaluation in genetic programming in particular. Most approaches compile linear or tree programs on the host PC and transfer the executable to the GPU to be run. Typically the performance advantage is only obtained by running the single active program simultaneously on many example problems in parallel, using the GPU's SIMD architecture.[21] [22] However, substantial acceleration can also be obtained by not compiling the programs, and instead transferring them to the GPU, to be interpreted there.[23] [24] Acceleration can then be obtained by either interpreting multiple programs simultaneously, simultaneously running multiple example problems, or combinations of both. A modern GPU (*e.g.* 8800 GTX or later) can readily simultaneously interpret hundreds of thousands of very small programs.

See also

Reference

- Brute force attack
- Computer graphics
- Computer hardware
- Computer monitor
- Central processing unit
- Physics processing unit (PPU)
- Ray tracing hardware
- Video card
- Video Display Controller
- Video game console

Hardware

- Comparison of AMD graphics processing units
- Comparison of Nvidia graphics processing units
- Intel GMA
- Larrabee
- Nvidia PureVideo - the bit-stream technology from Nvidia used in their graphics chips to accelerate video decoding on hardware GPU with DXVA.
- UVD (Unified Video Decoder) - is the video decoding bit-stream technology from ATI Technologies to support hardware (GPU) decode with DXVA.

APIs

- DirectX Video Acceleration (DxVA) API for Microsoft Windows operating-system.
- OpenVideo Decode (OVD) – an new open cross-platform video acceleration API from AMD.[25]
- Video Acceleration API (VA API)
- Video Decode Acceleration Framework is Apple Inc.s API for hardware-accelerated decoding of H.264 on Mac OS X
- VDPAU (Video Decode and Presentation API for Unix)
- VideoToolBox is an undocumented API from Apple Inc. for hardware-accelerated decoding on Apple TV and Mac OS X 10.5 or later.[26]
- X-Video Bitstream Acceleration (XvBA), the X11 equivalent of DXVA for MPEG-2, H.264, and VC-1
- X-Video Motion Compensation, the X11 equivalent for MPEG-2 video codec only

Applications

- GPU cluster
- NCLab provides free GPU programming in the web browser.
- Mathematica includes built-in support for CUDA and OpenCL GPU execution
- MATLAB acceleration using the Parallel Computing Toolbox and MATLAB Distributed Computing Server,[27] as well as 3rd party packages like Jacket.
- Molecular modeling on GPU
- Bitcoin Mining

References

[1] Denny Atkin. "Computer Shopper: The Right GPU for You" (http://computershopper.com/feature/200704_the_right_gpu_for_you). . Retrieved 2007-05-15.

[2] Michael Swaine, "New Chip from Intel Gives High-Quality Displays", March 14, 1983, p.16

[3] 3dfx Glide API

[4] Søren Dreijer. "Bump Mapping Using CG (3rd Edition)" (http://www.blacksmith-studios.dk/projects/downloads/ bumpmapping_using_cg.php). . Retrieved 2007-05-30.

[5] http://www.xbitlabs.com/articles/video/display/power-noise.html X-bit labs: Faster, Quieter, Lower: Power Consumption and Noise Level of Contemporary Graphics Cards

[6] http://dl.acm.org/citation.cfm?id=1553486

[7] "Linear algebra operators for GPU implementation of numerical algorithms", Kruger and Westermann, International Conf. on Computer Graphics and Interactive Techniques, 2005

[8] "ABC-SysBio—approximate Bayesian computation in Python with GPU support", Liepe et al., Bioinformatics, (2010), 26:1797-1799 (http:// bioinformatics.oxfordjournals.org/content/26/14/1797.full)

[9] Khronos Group (http://www.khronos.org/opencl/)

[10] Q3 Sales Report from Jon Peddie Research via TechReport.com (http://techreport.com/discussions.x/15778)

[11] http://www.s3graphics.com/en/products/index.aspx

[12] http://www.via.com.tw/en/products/graphics

[13] http://www.matrox.com/graphics/en/products/graphics_cards

[14] AnandTech: µATX Part 2: Intel G33 Performance Review (http://www.anandtech.com/mb/showdoc.aspx?i=3111&p=23)

[15] Tim Tscheblockov. "Xbit Labs: Roundup of 7 Contemporary Integrated Graphics Chipsets for Socket 478 and Socket A Platforms" (http:// www.xbitlabs.com/articles/chipsets/display/int-chipsets-roundup.html). . Retrieved 2007-06-03.

[16] Bradley Sanford. "Integrated Graphics Solutions for Graphics-Intensive Applications" (http://www.amd.com/us-en/assets/content_type/ white_papers_and_tech_docs/Integrated_Graphics_Solutions_white_paper_rev61.pdf). . Retrieved 2007-09-02.

[17] Bradley Sanford. "Integrated Graphics Solutions for Graphics-Intensive Applications" (http://www.techspot.com/news/ 46773-amd-announces-radeon-hd-7970-claims-fastest-gpu-title.html). . Retrieved 2007-09-02.

[18] Darren Murph. "Stanford University tailors Folding@home to GPUs" (http://www.engadget.com/2006/09/29/ stanford-university-tailors-folding-home-to-gpus/). . Retrieved 2007-10-04.

[19] Mike Houston. "Folding@Home - GPGPU" (http://graphics.stanford.edu/~mhouston/). . Retrieved 2007-10-04.

[20] http://pressroom.nvidia.com/easyir/customrel.do?easyirid=A0D622CE9F579F09&version=live&prid=678988& releasejsp=release_157

[21] John Nickolls. "Stanford Lecture: Scalable Parallel Programming with CUDA on Manycore GPUs" (http://www.youtube.com/watch?v=nlGnKPpOpbE). .

[22] S Harding and W Banzhaf. "Fast genetic programming on GPUs" (http://www.cs.bham.ac.uk/~wbl/biblio/gp-html/eurogp07_harding.html). . Retrieved 2008-05-01.

[23] W Langdon and W Banzhaf. "A SIMD interpreter for Genetic Programming on GPU Graphics Cards" (http://www.cs.bham.ac.uk/~wbl/biblio/gp-html/langdon_2008_eurogp.html). . Retrieved 2008-05-01.

[24] V. Garcia and E. Debreuve and M. Barlaud. Fast k nearest neighbor search using GPU. In Proceedings of the CVPR Workshop on Computer Vision on GPU, Anchorage, Alaska, USA, June 2008.

[25] http://developer.amd.com/gpu/AMDAPPSDK/assets/OpenVideo_Decode_API.PDF OpenVideo Decode (OVD) API

[26] http://www.tuaw.com/2011/01/20/xbmc-for-ios-and-atv2-now-available/XBMC for iOS and Apple TV now available

[27] "MATLAB Adds GPGPU Support" (http://www.hpcwire.com/features/MATLAB-Adds-GPGPU-Support-103307084.html). 2010-09-20. .

External links

- GPU Specifications, Comparison, and Performance Charts (http://www.gpubench.com)
- NVIDIA - What is a GPU? (http://www.nvidia.com/content/nsist/module/what_gpu.asp)
- The *GPU Gems* book series (http://developer.nvidia.com/object/gpu_gems_2_home.html)
- - a Graphics Hardware History (http://titancity.com/articles/gfxcards.html)
- Toms Hardware GPU beginners' Guide (http://www.tomshardware.com/2006/08/08/graphics_beginners_3/)
- General-Purpose Computation Using Graphics Hardware (http://www.gpgpu.org/)
- How GPUs work (http://www.cs.virginia.edu/~gfx/papers/paper.php?paper_id=59)
- GPU Caps Viewer - Video card information utility (http://www.ozone3d.net/gpu_caps_viewer/)
- OpenGPU-GPU Architecture(In Chinese) (http://www.opengpu.org/bbs/index.php)
- ARM Mali GPUs Overview (http://www.malideveloper.com/mali/index.php)

Performance_per_watt

In computing, **performance per watt** is a measure of the energy efficiency of a particular computer architecture or computer hardware. Literally, it measures the rate of computation that can be delivered by a computer for every watt of power consumed.

The performance and power consumption metrics used depend on the definition; reasonable measures of performance are FLOPS, MIPS, or the score for any performance benchmark. Several measures of power usage may be employed, depending on the purposes of the metric; for example, a metric might only consider the electrical power delivered to a machine directly, while another might include all power necessary to run a computer, such as cooling and monitoring systems. Often the power is the average power used while running the benchmark, but sometimes other measures of power usage may be employed (e.g. peak power, idle power.)

For example, the early UNIVAC I computer performed approximately 0.015 operations per watt-second (performing 1,905 operations per second, while consuming 125 kW).

Most of the power a computer uses is converted into heat, so a system that takes fewer watts to do a job will require less cooling to maintain a given operating temperature. Reduced cooling demands makes it easier to quieten a computer. Lower energy consumption can also make it less costly to run, and reduce the environmental impact of powering the computer (see green computing). If installed where there is limited climate control, a lower power computer will operate at a lower temperature, which may make it more reliable. In a climate controlled environment, reductions in direct power use may also create savings in climate control energy.

Computing energy consumption is sometimes also measured by reporting the energy required to run a particular benchmark, for instance EEMBC EnergyBench. Energy consumption figures for a standard workload may make it easier to judge the effect of an improvement in energy efficiency, just as the use of L/100km is easier than reciprocal measures (such as miles per gallon) when judging impact of automotive fuel economy.

Performance (in operations/second) per watt can also be written as operations/watt-second, or operations/joule, since 1 watt = 1 joule/second.

FLOPS per watt

FLOPS (Floating Point Operations Per Second) **per watt** is a common measure. Like the FLOPS it is based on, the metric is usually applied to scientific computing and simulations involving many floating point calculations.

Examples

As of June 2011, the Green500 list rates IBM NNSA/SC Blue Gene/Q Prototype 2 as the most efficient supercomputer on the TOP500 in terms of FLOPS per Watt, running at 2097.19 MFLOPS/Watt.[1]

On 9 June 2008, CNN reported that IBM's Roadrunner supercomputer achieves 376 MFLOPS/Watt.[2] [3] In November 2010, IBM machine, Blue Gene/Q achieves 1684 MFLOPS/Watt. [4] [5]

As part of Intel's Tera-Scale research project, the team produced an 80 core CPU that can achieve over 16 GFLOPS/Watt.[6] [7] The future of that CPU is not certain.

Microwulf, a low cost desktop Beowulf cluster of 4 dual core Athlon 64 x2 3800+ computers, runs at 58 MFLOPS/Watt.[8]

Green500 List

The Green500 list ranks computers from the TOP500 list of supercomputers in terms of energy efficiency. Typically measured as LINPACK FLOPS per watt.[9] [10]

GPU efficiency

Graphics processing units (GPU) have continued to increase in energy usage, while CPUs designers have recently focused on improving performance per watt. High performance GPUs may now be the largest power consumer in a system. Measures like 3DMark2006 score per watt can help identify more efficient GPUs.[11] However that may not adequately incorporate efficiency in typical use, where much time is spent doing less demanding tasks.[12]

With modern GPUs, energy usage is an important constraint on the possible power. GPU designs are usually highly scalable, allowing the manufacturer to put multiple chips on the same video card, or to use multiple video cards that work in parallel. Peak performance of any system is essentially limited by the amount of power it can draw and the amount of heat it can dissipate. Consequently, performance per watt of a GPU design translates directly into peak performance of a system that uses that design.

Since GPUs may also be used for some general purpose computation, sometimes their performance is measured in terms also applied to CPUs, such as FLOPS per watt.

Challenges

While performance per watt is useful, absolute power requirements are also important. Claims of improved performance per watt may be used to mask increasing power demands. For instance, though newer generation GPU architectures may provide better performance per watt, continued performance increases can negate the gains in efficiency, and the GPUs continue to consume large amounts of power.[13] .

Benchmarks that measure power under heavy load may not adequately reflect typical efficiency. For instance, 3DMark stresses the 3D performance of a GPU, but many computers spend most of their time doing less intense display tasks (idle, 2D tasks, displaying video). So the 2D or idle efficiency of the graphics system may be at least as significant for overall energy efficiency. Likewise, systems that spend much of their time in standby or soft off are not adequately characterized by just efficiency under load. To help address this some benchmarks, like SPECpower, include measurements at a series of load levels.[14]

The efficiency of some electrical components, such as voltage regulators, decreases with increasing temperature, so the power used may increase with temperature. Power supplies, motherboards, and some video cards are some of the subsystems affected by this. So their power draw may depend on temperature, and the temperature or temperature dependence should be noted when measuring.[15] [16]

Performance per watt also typically does not include full life-cycle costs. Since computer manufacturing is energy intensive, and computers often have a relatively short lifespan, energy and materials involved in production, distribution, disposal and recycling often make up significant portions of their cost, energy use, and environmental impact.[17] [18]

Energy required for climate control of the computer's surroundings is often not counted in the wattage calculation, but can be significant.[19]

Other energy efficiency measures

SWaP (space, wattage and performance) is a Sun Microsystems metric for data centers, incorporating energy and space.

SWaP = Performance/(Space x Power)

Where performance is measured by any appropriate benchmark, and space is size of the computer. [20]

See also

Energy efficiency benchmarks:

- Average CPU Power Measures power used running several standard benchmarks.
- SPECpower Benchmark for web servers running Java. (Server Side Java Operations per Joule)
- EEMBC EnergyBench.

Other:

- GeForce 9 Series GPU list, has energy use and theoretical FLOPS.
- Power usage effectiveness (PUE)
- Data center infrastructure efficiency (DCIE)
- low-power electronics
- IT energy management

References

[1] "The Green500 List" (http://www.green500.org/lists/2011/06/top/list.php?from=1&to=100). *Green500.* .

[2] "Government unveils world's fastest computer" (http://web.archive.org/web/20080610155646/http://www.cnn.com/2008/TECH/06/
     09/fastest.computer.ap/index.html). *CNN.* Archived from the original (http://www.cnn.com/2008/TECH/06/09/fastest.computer.ap/
     index.html) on 2008-06-10. . "performing 376 million calculations for every watt of electricity used."

[3] "IBM Roadrunner Takes the Gold in the Petaflop Race" (http://www.hpcwire.com/topic/processors/
     IBM_Roadrunner_Takes_the_Gold_in_the_Petaflop_Race.html). .

[4] "Top500 Supercomputing List Reveals Computing Trends" (http://www.serverwatch.com/hreviews/article.php/3913536/
     Top500-Supercomputing-List-Reveals-Computing-Trends.htm). . "IBM... BlueGene/Q system .. setting a record in power efficiency with a
     value of 1,680 Mflops/watt, more than twice that of the next best system."

[5] "IBM Research A Clear Winner in Green 500" (http://www.datacenterknowledge.com/archives/2010/11/18/
     ibm-system-clear-winner-in-green-500/). .

[6] "Intel squeezes 1.8 TFlops out of one processor" (http://www.tgdaily.com/content/view/30929/135/). *TG Daily.* .

[7] "Teraflops Research Chip" (http://techresearch.intel.com/articles/Tera-Scale/1449.htm). *Intel Technology and Research.* .

[8] Joel Adams. "Microwulf: Power Efficiency" (http://www.calvin.edu/~adams/research/microwulf/power/). *Microwulf: A Personal,
     Portable Beowulf Cluster.* .

[9] "The Green 500" (http://www.green500.org). .

[10] "Green 500 list ranks supercomputers" (http://www.itnews.com.au/News/65619,green-500-list-ranks-supercomputers.aspx). *iTnews
     Australia.* .

[11] Atwood, Jeff (2006-08-18). "Video Card Power Consumption" (http://www.codinghorror.com/blog/archives/000662.html). .

[12] "Video card power consumption" (http://www.xbitlabs.com/articles/video/display/power-noise.html). *Xbit Labs.* .

[13] Tim Smalley. "Performance per What?" (http://www.bit-tech.net/columns/2007/05/20/performance_per_what/1). *Bit Tech.* . Retrieved
     2008-04-21.

[14] "SPEC launches standardized energy efficiency benchmark" (http://blogs.zdnet.com/Ou/?p=927). *ZDNet.* .

[15] Mike Chin. "Asus EN9600GT Silent Edition Graphics Card" (http://www.silentpcreview.com/article821-page5.html). *Silent PC Review.*
     p. 5. . Retrieved 2008-04-21.

[16] MIke Chin. "80 Plus expands podium for Bronze, Silver & Gold" (http://www.silentpcreview.com/article814-page1.html). *Silent PC
     Review.* . Retrieved 2008-04-21.

[17] Mike Chin. "Life Cycle Analysis and Eco PC Review" (http://www.ecopcreview.com/LCA_and_ECPR). *Eco PC Review.* .

[18] Eric Williams (2004). "Energy intensity of computer manufacturing: hybrid assessment combining process and economic input-output
     methods" (http://pubs.acs.org/cgi-bin/abstract.cgi/esthag/2004/38/i22/abs/es035152j.html). *Environ. Sci. Technol.* **38** (22): 6166.
     doi:10.1021/es035152j. PMID 15573621. .

[19] Wu-chun Feng (2005). "The Importance of Being Low Power in High Performance Computing" (http://www.ctwatch.org/quarterly/
     articles/2005/08/the-importance-of-being-low-power-in-high-performance-computing/). *CT Watch Quarterly* **1** (5). .

[20] "Sun SWaP: Metric for server efficiency and datacenter systems" (http://www.webhostingjournal.net/archives/
     Sun-SWaP-Metric-for-server-efficiency-and-datacenter-systems/#content). *Web Hosting Journal.* 6 december 2005. .

Further reading

- Wu-Chun Feng (October 2003). "Making a case for Efficient Supercomputing" (http://www.acmqueue.com/
  modules.php?name=Content&pa=showpage&pid=80&page=1). *ACM Queue* **1** (7).

External links

- 25 Energy Efficient Supercomputers (http://www.eweek.com/c/a/Green-IT/
  Top-25-Most-Energy-Efficient-Supercomputers/)
- The Green 500 list (http://www.green500.org)

FLOPS

Computer performance

Name	FLOPS
yottaFLOPS	10^{24}
zettaFLOPS	10^{21}
exaFLOPS	10^{18}
petaFLOPS	10^{15}
teraFLOPS	10^{12}
gigaFLOPS	10^{9}
megaFLOPS	10^{6}
kiloFLOPS	10^{3}

In computing, **FLOPS** (or **flops** or **flop/s**, for **floating-point operations per second**) is a measure of a computer's performance, especially in fields of scientific calculations that make heavy use of floating-point calculations, similar to the older, simpler, instructions per second. Since the final S stands for "second", conservative speakers consider "FLOPS" as both the singular and plural of the term, although the singular "FLOP" is frequently encountered. Alternatively, the singular **FLOP** (or **flop**) is used as an abbreviation for "**FL**oating-point **OP**eration", and a flop count is a count of these operations (e.g., required by a given algorithm or computer program). In this context, "flops" is simply the plural rather than a rate.

Although it is in common use, FLOPS is not an SI unit. The expression 1 flops is actually interpreted as .

Measuring performance

In order for FLOPS to be useful as a measure of floating-point performance, a standard benchmark must be available on all computers of interest. One example is the LINPACK benchmark.

There are many factors in computer performance other than raw floating-point computing speed, such as I/O performance, interprocessor communication, cache coherence, and the memory hierarchy. This means that supercomputers are in general only capable of a fraction of their "theoretical peak" FLOPS throughput (obtained by adding together the theoretical peak FLOPS performance of every element of the system). Even when operating on large highly parallel problems, their performance will be bursty, mostly due to the residual effects of Amdahl's law. Real benchmarks therefore measure both peak actual FLOPS performance as well as sustained FLOPS performance.

Supercomputer ratings, like TOP500, usually derive theoretical peak FLOPS as a product of number of cores, cycles per second each core runs at, and number of double-precision (64 bit) FLOPS each core can ideally perform, thanks to SIMD or otherwise. Despite different processor architectures can achieve different parallelism on single core, most mainstream ones, like recent Xeon and Itanium models, claim a factor of four. Some ratings adopted the factor as a given constant, and use it to compute peak values for all architectures, often leading to huge difference from sustained performance.

For ordinary (non-scientific) applications, integer operations (measured in MIPS) are far more common. Measuring floating-point operation speed, therefore, does not predict accurately how the processor will perform on just any problem. However, for many scientific jobs such as data analysis, a FLOPS rating is effective.

Historically, the earliest reliably documented serious use of the floating-point operation as a metric appears to be AEC justification to Congress for purchasing a Control Data CDC 6600 in the mid-1960s.

The terminology is currently so confusing that until April 24, 2006, U.S. export control was based upon measurement of "Composite Theoretical Performance" (CTP) in millions of "Theoretical Operations Per Second" or MTOPS. On that date, however, the U.S. Department of Commerce's Bureau of Industry and Security amended the Export Administration Regulations to base controls on Adjusted Peak Performance (APP) in Weighted TeraFLOPS (WT).

Records

NEC's SX-9 supercomputer was the world's first vector processor to exceed 100 gigaFLOPS per single core. IBM's supercomputer dubbed Roadrunner was the first to reach a sustained performance of 1 petaFLOPS, as measured by the Linpack benchmark. As of June 2011, the 500 fastest supercomputers in the world combine for 58.9 petaFLOPS of computing power.[1]

For comparison, a hand-held calculator performs relatively few FLOPS. Each calculation request, such as to add or subtract two numbers, requires only a single operation, so there is rarely any need for its response time to exceed what the operator can physically use. A computer response time below 0.1 second in a calculation context is usually perceived as instantaneous by a human operator,[2] so a simple calculator needs only about 10 FLOPS to be considered functional.

In June 2006, a new computer was announced by Japanese research institute RIKEN, the MDGRAPE-3. The computer's performance tops out at one petaFLOPS, almost two times faster than the Blue Gene/L, but MDGRAPE-3 is not a general purpose computer, which is why it does not appear in the Top500.org list. It has special-purpose pipelines for simulating molecular dynamics.

By 2007, Intel Corporation unveiled the experimental multi-core POLARIS chip, which achieves 1 TFLOPS at 3.13 GHz. The 80-core chip can raise this result to 2 TFLOPS at 6.26 GHz, although the thermal dissipation at this frequency exceeds 190 watts.[3]

On June 26, 2007, IBM announced the second generation of its top supercomputer, dubbed Blue Gene/P and designed to continuously operate at speeds exceeding one petaFLOPS. When configured to do so, it can reach speeds in excess of three petaFLOPS.[4]

In June 2007, Top500.org reported the fastest computer in the world to be the IBM Blue Gene/L supercomputer, measuring a peak of 596 TFLOPS.[5] The Cray XT4 hit second place with 101.7 TFLOPS.

On October 25, 2007, NEC Corporation of Japan issued a press release[6] announcing its SX series model SX-9, claiming it to be the world's fastest vector supercomputer. The SX-9 features the first CPU capable of a peak vector performance of 102.4 gigaFLOPS per single core.

On February 4, 2008, the NSF and the University of Texas opened full scale research runs on an AMD, Sun supercomputer named Ranger,[7] the most powerful supercomputing system in the world for open science research, which operates at sustained speed of half a petaFLOPS.

On May 25, 2008, an American supercomputer built by IBM, named 'Roadrunner', reached the computing milestone of one petaflop by processing more than 1.026 quadrillion calculations per second. It headed the June 2008[8] and November 2008[9] TOP500 list of the most powerful supercomputers (excluding grid computers). The computer is located at Los Alamos National Laboratory in New Mexico, and the computer's name refers to the New Mexico state bird, the Greater Roadrunner.[10]

In June 2008, AMD released ATI Radeon HD4800 series, which are reported to be the first GPUs to achieve one teraFLOPS scale. On August 12, 2008 AMD released the ATI Radeon HD 4870X2 graphics card with two Radeon R770 GPUs totaling 2.4 teraFLOPS.

In November 2008, an upgrade to the Cray XT Jaguar supercomputer at the Department of Energy's (DOE's) Oak Ridge National Laboratory (ORNL) raised the system's computing power to a peak 1.64 "petaflops," or a quadrillion mathematical calculations per second, making Jaguar the world's first petaflop system dedicated to open research. In early 2009 the supercomputer was named after a mythical creature, Kraken. Kraken was declared the world's fastest university-managed supercomputer and sixth fastest overall in the 2009 TOP500 list, which is the global standard for ranking supercomputers. In 2010 Kraken was upgraded and can operate faster and is more powerful.

In 2009, the Cray Jaguar performed at 1.75 petaFLOPS, beating the IBM Roadrunner for the number one spot on the TOP500 list.[11]

In October 2010, China unveiled the Tianhe-I, a supercomputer that operates at a peak computing rate of 2.5 petaflops.[12] [13]

As of 2010, the fastest six-core PC processor reaches 109 GFLOPS (Intel Core i7 980 XE)[14] in double precision calculations. GPUs are considerably more powerful. For example, Nvidia Tesla C2050 GPU computing processors perform around 515 GFLOPS[15] in double precision calculations, and the AMD FireStream 9270 peaks at 240 GFLOPS.[16] In single precision performance, Nvidia Tesla C2050 computing processors perform around 1.03 TFLOPS and the AMD FireStream 9270 cards peak at 1.2 TFLOPS. Both Nvidia and AMD's consumer gaming GPUs may reach higher FLOPS. For example, AMD's HemlockXT 5970[17] reaches 928 GFLOPS in double precision calculations with two GPUs on board and the Nvidia GTX 480 reaches 672 GFLOPS[18] with one GPU on board.

In November 2011, it was announced that Japan had achieved 10.51 petaflops with its K computer.[19] It is still under development and software performance tuning is currently underway. It has 88,128 SPARC64 VIIIfx processors in 864 racks, with theoretical performance of 11.28 petaflops. It is named after the Japanese word "kei", which stands for 10 quadrillion,[20] corresponding to the target speed of 10 petaFLOPS.

On November 15, 2011, Intel demonstrated a single x86-based processor, code-named "Knights Corner," sustaining more than a TeraFlop on a wide range of DGEMM operations. Intel emphasized during the demonstration this was a sustained TeraFlop (not "raw TeraFlop" used by others to get higher but less meaningful numbers), and that it was the first general purpose processor to ever cross a TeraFlop.[21] [22]

Distributed computing uses the Internet to link personal computers to achieve more FLOPS:

- Folding@home is sustaining over 5.6 native petaFLOPS as of March 2012[23] or 8.1 x86 PFLOPS (x86 flops are an approximate measurement of the speed of a calculation on an x86-based processor, different from native flops[24]). It is the first computing project of any kind to cross the 1, 2, 3, 4, and 5 native petaFLOPS milestone. This level of performance is primarily enabled by the cumulative effort of a vast array of powerful GPU, PlayStation 3 and CPU units.[25]
- The entire BOINC network averages about 6.1 PFLOPS as of April 15, 2012.[26]
- As of April 2012, MilkyWay@Home computes at over 700 TFLOPS, with a large amount of this work coming from GPUs.[27]
- As of April 2012, SETI@Home, which began in 1999, computes data averages more than 540 TFLOPS.[28]
- As of April 2012, Einstein@Home is crunching more than 260 TFLOPS.[29]
- As of April 2012, GIMPS, which began in 1996, is sustaining 81 TFLOPS.[30]

Future developments

In 2008, James Bamford's The Shadow Factory reported that NSA told the Pentagon it would need an exaflop computer by 2018.[31]

In May 2008, a collaboration was announced between NASA, SGI, and Intel to build a 1 PFLOPS computer, Pleiades, in 2009, scaling up to 10 PFLOPS by 2012.[32] At the same time, IBM intended to build a 20 PFLOPS supercomputer, Sequoia, at Lawrence Livermore National Laboratory until 2011.

On December 2, 2010, the US Air Force unveiled a defense supercomputer made up of 1,760 Playstation 3 consoles that can run 500 trillion floating-point operations per second.[33] (500 TFLOPS)

On October 11, 2011, the Oak Ridge National Laboratory announced it was building a 20 petaflop supercomputer, named Titan, which will become operational in 2012, the hybrid Titan system will combine AMD Opteron processors with "Kepler" NVIDIA Tesla graphic processing unit (GPU) technologies.[34]

Given the current speed of progress, supercomputers are projected to reach 1 exaFLOPS (EFLOPS) in 2019.[35] Cray, Inc. announced in December 2009 a plan to build a 1 EFLOPS supercomputer before 2020.[36] Erik P. DeBenedictis of Sandia National Laboratories theorizes that a zettaFLOPS (ZFLOPS) computer is required to accomplish full weather modeling of two week time span.[37] Such systems might be built around 2030.[38]

In India, ISRO and Indian Institute of Science have planned to make a 132.8 exaflop supercomputer by 2017, 100 times faster than any supercomputer ever planned. It would cost US $2 billion, but the Indian Government is ready to provide funding and all key equipment is booked. ISRO Scientists say they have planned very carefully to put up such a target.[39]

Cost of computing

Hardware costs

The following is a list of examples of computers that demonstrates how drastically performance has increased and price has decreased. The "cost per GFLOPS" is the cost for a set of hardware that would theoretically operate at one billion floating-point operations per second. During the era when no single computing platform was able to achieve one GFLOPS, this table lists the total cost for multiple instances of a fast computing platform which speed sums to one GFLOPS. Otherwise, the least expensive computing platform able to achieve one GFLOPS is listed.

Date	Approximate cost per GFLOPS	Technology	Comments
1961	US $1,100,000,000,000 ($1.1 trillion)	About 17 million IBM 1620 units costing $64,000 each	The 1620's multiplication operation takes 17.7 ms.[40]
1984	$15,000,000	Cray X-MP	
1997	$30,000	Two 16-processor Beowulf clusters with Pentium Pro microprocessors[41]	
April 2000	$1,000	Bunyip Beowulf cluster[42]	Bunyip was the first sub-US$1/MFLOPS computing technology. It won the Gordon Bell Prize in 2000.
May 2000	$640	KLAT2[43]	KLAT2 was the first computing technology which scaled to large applications while staying under US$1/MFLOPS.[44]
August 2003	$82	KASY0[45]	KASY0 was the first sub-US$100/GFLOPS computing technology.[46]
August 2007	$48	Microwulf[47]	As of August 2007, this 26.25 GFLOPS "personal" Beowulf cluster can be built for $1256.[48]

March 2011	$1.80	HPU4Science [49]	This $30,000 cluster was built using only commercially available "gamer" grade hardware. [50]

The trend toward placing ever more transistors inexpensively on an integrated circuit follows Moore's law. This trend explains the rising speed and falling cost of computer processing.

Operation costs

In energy cost, according to the Green500 list, as of June 2011 the most efficient TOP500 supercomputer runs at 2097.19 MFLOPS per watt. This translates to an energy requirement of 0.477 watts per GFLOPS, however this energy requirement will be much greater for less efficient supercomputers.

Hardware costs for low cost supercomputers may be less significant than energy costs when running continuously for several years.

Floating-point operation and integer operation

Floating-point operation per second or FLOPS, measures the computing ability of a computer. An example of a floating-point operation is the calculation of mathematical equations. FLOPS is a good indicator to measure performance on DSP, supercomputers, robotic motion control, and scientific simulations. MIPS is used to measure the integer performance of a computer. Examples of integer operation is data movement (A to B) or value testing (If A = B, then C). MIPS as a performance benchmark is adequate for the computer when it is used in database query, word processing, spreadsheets, or to run multiple virtual operating systems.[51] [52] Frank H. McMahon, of the Lawrence Livermore National Laboratory (LLNL), invented the term FLOPS and MFLOPS (MegaFLOPS) so that he could compare the so-called Supercomputers of the day by the number of floating-point calculations they did per second. This was much better than using the prevalent MIPS (Millions of Instructions Per Second) to compare computers as this statistic usually had little bearing on the arithmetic capability of the machine.

Fixed-point (integers). These designations refer to the format used to store and manipulate numeric representations of data. Fixed-point are designed to represent and manipulate integers – positive and negative whole numbers – for example 16 bits, yielding up to 65,536 possible bit patterns (2^{16}).[53]

Floating-point (real numbers). The encoding scheme for floating-point numbers is more complicated than for fixed-point. The basic idea is the same as used in scientific notation, where a mantissa is multiplied by ten raised to some exponent. For instance, 5.4321×10^6, where 5.4321 is the mantissa and 6 is the exponent. Scientific notation is exceptional at representing very large and very small numbers. For example: 1.2×10^{50}, the number of atoms in the earth, or 2.6×10^{-23}, the distance a turtle crawls in one second compared to the diameter of our galaxy. Notice that numbers represented in scientific notation are normalized so that there is only a single nonzero digit left of the decimal point. This is achieved by adjusting the exponent as needed. Floating-point representation is similar to scientific notation, except everything is carried out in base two, rather than base ten. While several similar formats are in use, the most common is ANSI/IEEE Std. 754-1985. This standard defines the format for 32-bit numbers called *single precision*, as well as 64-bit numbers called *double precision* and longer numbers called *extended precision* (used for intermediate results). Floating-point representations can support a much wider range of values than fixed-point, with the ability to represent very small numbers and very large numbers.

With fixed-point notation, the gaps between adjacent numbers always equal a value of one, whereas in floating-point notation, gaps between adjacent numbers are not uniformly spaced—the gap between any two numbers is approximately ten million times smaller than the value of the numbers (ANSI/IEEE Std. 754 standard format), with large gaps between large numbers and small gaps between small numbers.[54]

Dynamic range and precision. The exponentiation inherent in floating-point computation assures a much larger dynamic range – the largest and smallest numbers that can be represented - which is especially important when processing data sets which are extremely large or where the range may be unpredictable. As such, floating-point processors are ideally suited for computationally intensive applications. It is also important to consider fixed and floating-point formats in the context of precision — the size of the gaps between numbers. Every time a processor generates a new number via a mathematical calculation, that number must be rounded to the nearest value that can be stored via the format in use. Rounding and/or truncating numbers during processing naturally yields quantization error or 'noise' - the deviation between actual values and quantized values. Since the gaps between adjacent numbers can be much larger with fixed-point processing when compared to floating-point processing, round-off error can be much more pronounced. As such, floating-point processing yields much greater precision than fixed-point processing, distinguishing floating-point processors as the ideal CPU when computing accuracy is a critical requirement.[55]

See also

- Gordon Bell Prize
- Orders of magnitude (computing)

References

[1] "Number of Processors share for 06/2011" (http://www.top500.org/stats/list/37/procclass). *TOP500 Supercomputing Site.* . Retrieved June 23, 2011

[2] "Response Times: The Three Important Limits" (http://www.useit.com/papers/responsetime.html). Jakob Nielsen. . Retrieved June 11, 2008.

[3] Published on 30th April 2007 by Richard Swinburne (2007-04-30), *The Arrival of TeraFLOP Computing* (http://www.bit-tech.net/hardware/2007/04/30/the_arrival_of_teraflop_computing/2), bit-tech.net, , retrieved 2012-02-09

[4] "June 2008" (http://www.top500.org/lists/2008/06). TOP500. . Retrieved July 8, 2008.

[5] "29th TOP500 List of World's Fastest Supercomputers Released" (http://top500.org/news/2007/06/23/29th_top500_list_world_s_fastest_supercomputers_released). Top500.org. June 23, 2007. . Retrieved July 8, 2008.

[6] "NEC Launches World's Fastest Vector Supercomputer, SX-9" (http://www.nec.co.jp/press/en/0710/2501.html). NEC. October 25, 2007. . Retrieved July 8, 2008.

[7] "University of Texas at Austin, Texas Advanced Computing Center" (http://www.tacc.utexas.edu/resources/hpcsystems/). . Retrieved September 13, 2010. "Any researcher at a U.S. institution can submit a proposal to request an allocation of cycles on the system."

[8] Sharon Gaudin (June 9, 2008). "IBM's Roadrunner smashes 4-minute mile of supercomputing" (http://www.computerworld.com/action/article.do?command=viewArticleBasic&taxonomyName=hardware&articleId=9095318&taxonomyId=12&intsrc=kc_top). Computerworld. . Retrieved June 10, 2008.

[9] *Austin ISC08* (http://www.top500.org/lists/2008/11/press-release), Top500.org, 2008-11-14, , retrieved 2012-02-09

[10] Fildes, Jonathan (June 9, 2008). "Supercomputer sets petaflop pace" (http://news.bbc.co.uk/1/hi/technology/7443557.stm). BBC News. . Retrieved July 8, 2008.

[11] Greenberg, Andy (November 16, 2009). "Cray Dethrones IBM In Supercomputing" (http://www.forbes.com/2009/11/15/supercomputer-ibm-jaguar-technology-cio-network-cray.html?feed=rss_popstories). *Forbes.* .

[12] "China claims supercomputer crown" (http://www.bbc.co.uk/news/technology-11644252). *BBC News.* October 28, 2010. .

[13] Dillow, Clay (2010-10-28), *China Unveils 2507 Petaflop Supercomputer, the World's Fastest* (http://www.popsci.com/technology/article/2010-10/china-unveils-2507-petaflop-supercomputer-worlds-fastest), Popsci.com, , retrieved 2012-02-09

[14] *Intel's Core i7-980X Extreme Edition - Ready for Sick Scores?: Mathematics: Sandra Arithmetic, Crypto, Microsoft Excel* (http://techgage.com/article/intels_core_i7-980x_extreme_edition_-_ready_for_sick_scores/8), Techgage, 2010-03-10, , retrieved 2012-02-09

[15] *NVIDIA Tesla Personal Supercomputer* (http://www.nvidia.com/object/product_tesla_C2050_C2070_us.html), Nvidia.com, , retrieved 2012-02-09

[16] *AMD FireStream 9270 GPU Compute Accelerator* (http://www.amd.com/us/products/workstation/firestream/firestream-9270/pages/firestream-9270.aspx), Amd.com, , retrieved 2012-02-09

[17] http://www.amd.com/us/products/desktop/graphics/ati-radeon-hd-5000/hd-5970/Pages/ati-radeon-hd-5970-specifications.aspx

[18] *GeForce GTX 480* (http://www.nvidia.com/object/product_geforce_gtx_480_us.html), Nvidia.com, 2010-07-20, , retrieved 2012-02-09

[19] *"K computer" Achieves Goal of 10 Petaflops* (http://www.fujitsu.com/global/news/pr/archives/month/2011/20111102-02.html), Fujitsu.com, , retrieved 2012-02-09

[20] See Japanese numbers

[21] "Intel's Knights Corner: 50+ Core 22nm Co-processor" (http://www.tomshardware.com/news/intel-knights-corner-mic-co-processor,14002.html). . Retrieved November 16, 2011.

[22] "Intel unveils 1 TFLOP/s Knight's Corner" (http://www.eetimes.com/electronics-news/4230654/Intel-unveils-1-TFLOP-s-Knight-s-Corner). . Retrieved November 16, 2011.

[23] "Client statistics by OS" (http://fah-web.stanford.edu/cgi-bin/main.py?qtype=osstats). Folding@Home. March 11, 2012. . Retrieved March 11, 2012.

[24] "FLOP FAQ" (http://folding.stanford.edu/English/FAQ-flops). Folding@Home. April 4, 2009. . Retrieved March 11, 2012.

[25] Staff (November 6, 2008). "Sony Computer Entertainment's Support for Folding@home Project on PlayStation3 Receives This Year's "Good Design Gold Award"" (http://www.scei.co.jp/corporate/release/081106de.html). *Sony Computer Entertainment Inc.*. Sony Computer Entertainment Inc. (Sony Computer Entertainment Inc.). . Retrieved December 11, 2008.

[26] "Credit overview" (http://www.boincstats.com/stats/project_graph.php?pr=bo). BOINC. . Retrieved April 15, 2012.

[27] "MilkyWay@Home Credit overview" (http://boincstats.com/stats/project_graph.php?pr=milkyway). BOINC. . Retrieved April 15, 2012.

[28] "SETI@Home Credit overview" (http://www.boincstats.com/stats/project_graph.php?pr=sah). BOINC. . Retrieved April 15, 2012.

[29] "Einstein@Home Credit overview" (http://de.boincstats.com/stats/project_graph.php?pr=einstein). BOINC. . Retrieved April 15, 2012.

[30] "Internet PrimeNet Server Distributed Computing Technology for the Great Internet Mersenne Prime Search" (http://www.mersenne.org/primenet). *GIMPS*. . Retrieved April 15, 2012

[31] p339, Shadow Factory, Bamford

[32] "NASA collaborates with Intel and SGI on forthcoming petaflops super computers" (http://www.heise.de/english/newsticker/news/107683). *Heise online*. May 9, 2008. .

[33] Dillow, Clay, *Air Force Unveils Fastest Defense Supercomputer, Made of 1760 PlayStation 3* (http://www.popsci.com/technology/article/2010-12/air-forces-new-supercomputer-made-1760-playstation-3s), Popsci.com, , retrieved 2012-02-09

[34] Montalbano, Elizabeth (2011-10-11), *Oak Ridge Labs Builds Fastest Supercomputer* (http://www.informationweek.com/news/government/enterprise-architecture/231900554), Informationweek, , retrieved 2012-02-09

[35] Thibodeau, Patrick (June 10, 2008). "IBM breaks petaflop barrier" (http://www.infoworld.com/article/08/06/10/IBM_breaks_petaflop_barrier_1.html). *InfoWorld*. .

[36] *Cray studies exascale computing in Europe* (http://eetimes.com/news/latest/showArticle.jhtml?articleID=222000288), Eetimes.com, , retrieved 2012-02-09

[37] DeBenedictis, Erik P. (2005). "Reversible logic for supercomputing" (http://portal.acm.org/citation.cfm?id=1062325). *Proceedings of the 2nd conference on Computing frontiers*. New York, NY: ACM Press. pp. 391–402. ISBN 1-59593-019-1. .

[38] "IDF: Intel says Moore's Law holds until 2029" (http://www.h-online.com/newsticker/news/item/IDF-Intel-says-Moore-s-Law-holds-until-2029-734779.html). *Heise Online*. April 4, 2008. .

[39] "India to make World's Fastest Supercomputer" (http://www.defencenews.in/defence-news-internal.asp?get=new&id=500). .

[40] *IBM 1961 BRL Report* (http://ed-thelen.org/comp-hist/BRL61-ibm1401.html), Ed-thelen.org, , retrieved 2012-02-09

[41] *Loki and Hyglac* (http://loki-www.lanl.gov/papers/sc97/), Loki-www.lanl.gov, 1997-07-13, , retrieved 2012-02-09

[42] http://tsg.anu.edu.au/Projects/Beowulf/

[43] http://aggregate.org/KLAT2/

[44] *Kentucky Linux Athlon Testbed 2 (KLAT2)* (http://aggregate.org/KLAT2/), The Aggregate, , retrieved 2012-02-09

[45] http://aggregate.org/KASY0/

[46] *KASY0* (http://aggregate.org/KASY0/), The Aggregate, 2003-08-22, , retrieved 2012-02-09

[47] http://www.calvin.edu/~adams/research/microwulf/

[48] *Microwulf: A Personal, Portable Beowulf Cluster* (http://replay.waybackmachine.org/20070912061302/http://www.calvin.edu/~adams/research/microwulf/), Replay.waybackmachine.org, 2007-09-12, , retrieved 2012-02-09

[49] http://hpu4science.org

[50] Adam Stevenson, Yann Le Du, and Mariem El Afrit. " High-performance computing on gamer PCs (http://arstechnica.com/science/news/2011/03/high-performance-computing-on-gamer-pcs-part-1-hardware.ars)." *Ars Technica*. March 31, 2011.

[51] Fixed versus floating point. (http://www.dspguide.com/ch28/4.htm) Retrieved on December 25, 2009.

[52] Data manipulation and math calculation. (http://www.dspguide.com/ch28/1.htm) Retrieved on December 25, 2009.

[53] Integer (http://www.dspguide.com/ch4/2.htm) Retrieved on December 25, 2009.

[54] Floating Point (http://www.dspguide.com/ch4/3.htm) Retrieved on December 25, 2009.

[55] Summary: Fixed-point (integer) vs floating-point (http://www.analog.com/en/embedded-processing-dsp/content/Fixed-Point_vs_Floating-Point_DSP/fca.html) Retrieved on December 25, 2009.

External links

- Current Einstein@Home benchmark (http://einstein.phys.uwm.edu/server_status.php)
- BOINC projects global benchmark (http://www.boincstats.com/stats/project_graph.php?pr=bo)
- Current GIMPS throughput (http://mersenne.org/primenet/)
- Top500.org (http://top500.org)
- LinuxHPC.org (http://www.LinuxHPC.org) Linux High Performance Computing and Clustering Portal
- WinHPC.org (http://www.WinHPC.org) Windows High Performance Computing and Clustering Portal
- Oscar Linux-cluster ranking list by CPUs/types and respective FLOPS (http://svn.oscar.openclustergroup.org/php/clusters_register.php?sort=rpeak)
- Information on how to calculate "Composite Theoretical Performance" (CTP) (http://www.mosis.org/forms/mosis_forms/ECCN_CTP_Computation.pdf)
- Information on the Oak Ridge National Laboratory Cray XT system. (http://investors.cray.com/phoenix.zhtml?c=98390&p=irol-newsArticle&ID=873357&highlight=)
- Infiscale Cluster Portal - Free GPL HPC (http://www.perceus.org/portal/)
- Source code, pre-compiled versions and results for PCs (http://www.roylongbottom.org.uk/index.htm) - Linpack, Livermore Loops, Whetstone MFLOPS
- PC CPU Performance Comparisons %MFLOPS/MHz - CPU, Caches and RAM (http://www.roylongbottom.org.uk/cpuspeed.htm)
- Xeon export compliance metrics (http://www.intel.com/support/processors/xeon/sb/CS-020863.htm), including GFLOPS
- IBM Brings NVIDIA Tesla GPUs Onboard (May 2010) (http://www.hpcwire.com/features/IBM-Brings-NVIDIA-GPUs-Onboard-94190024.html)

Central_processing_unit

- An Intel 80486DX2 CPU from above - An Intel 80486DX2 from below The **central processing unit** (**CPU**) is the portion of a computer system that carries out the instructions of a computer program, to perform the basic arithmetical, logical, and input/output operations of the system. The CPU plays a role somewhat analogous to the brain in the computer. The term has been in use in the computer industry at least since the early 1960s.[1] The form, design and implementation of CPUs have changed dramatically since the earliest examples, but their fundamental operation remains much the same.

On large machines, CPUs require one or more printed circuit boards. On personal computers and small workstations, the CPU is housed in a single silicon chip called a microprocessor. Since the 1970s the microprocessor class of CPUs has almost completely overtaken all other CPU implementations. Modern CPUs are large scale integrated circuits in packages typically less than four centimeters square, with hundreds of connecting pins.

Two typical components of a CPU are the arithmetic logic unit (ALU), which performs arithmetic and logical operations, and the control unit (CU), which extracts instructions from memory and decodes and executes them, calling on the ALU when necessary.

Not all computational systems rely on a central processing unit. An array processor or vector processor has multiple parallel computing elements, with no one unit considered the "center". In the distributed computing model, problems are solved by a distributed interconnected set of processors.

History

Computers such as the ENIAC had to be physically rewired to perform different tasks, which caused these machines to be called "fixed-program computers." Since the term "CPU" is generally defined as a device for software (computer program) execution, the earliest devices that could rightly be called CPUs came with the advent of the stored-program computer.

The idea of a stored-program computer was already present in the design of J. Presper Eckert and John William Mauchly's ENIAC, but was initially omitted so that it could be finished sooner. On June 30, 1945, before ENIAC was made, mathematician John von Neumann distributed the paper entitled *First Draft of a Report on the EDVAC*. It was the outline of a stored-program computer that would eventually be completed in August 1949.[2] EDVAC was designed to perform a certain number of instructions (or operations) of various types. These instructions could be combined to create useful programs for the EDVAC to run. Significantly, the programs written for EDVAC were stored in high-speed computer memory rather than specified by the

EDVAC, one of the first stored program computers

physical wiring of the computer. This overcame a severe limitation of ENIAC, which was the considerable time and effort required to reconfigure the computer to perform a new task. With von Neumann's design, the program, or software, that EDVAC ran could be changed simply by changing the contents of the memory.

Early CPUs were custom-designed as a part of a larger, sometimes one-of-a-kind, computer. However, this method of designing custom CPUs for a particular application has largely given way to the development of mass-produced processors that are made for many purposes. This standardization began in the era of discrete transistor mainframes and minicomputers and has rapidly accelerated with the popularization of the integrated circuit (IC). The IC has allowed increasingly complex CPUs to be designed and manufactured to tolerances on the order of nanometers. Both the miniaturization and standardization of CPUs have increased the presence of digital devices in modern life far beyond the limited application of dedicated computing machines. Modern microprocessors appear in everything from automobiles to cell phones and children's toys.

While von Neumann is most often credited with the design of the stored-program computer because of his design of EDVAC, others before him, such as Konrad Zuse, had suggested and implemented similar ideas. The so-called Harvard architecture of the Harvard Mark I, which was completed before EDVAC, also utilized a stored-program design using punched paper tape rather than electronic memory. The key difference between the von Neumann and Harvard architectures is that the latter separates the storage and treatment of CPU instructions and data, while the former uses the same memory space for both. Most modern CPUs are primarily von Neumann in design, but elements of the Harvard architecture are commonly seen as well.

Relays and vacuum tubes (thermionic valves) were commonly used as switching elements; a useful computer requires thousands or tens of thousands of switching devices. The overall speed of a system is dependent on the speed of the switches. Tube computers like EDVAC tended to average eight hours between failures, whereas relay computers like the (slower, but earlier) Harvard Mark I failed very rarely.[1] In the end, tube based CPUs became dominant because the significant speed advantages afforded generally outweighed the reliability problems. Most of these early synchronous CPUs ran at low clock rates compared to modern microelectronic designs (see below for a discussion of clock rate). Clock signal frequencies ranging from 100 kHz to 4 MHz were very common at this time, limited largely by the speed of the switching devices they were built with.

Control unit

The control unit of the CPU contains circuitry that uses electrical signals to direct the entire computer system to carry out stored program instructions. The control unit does not execute program instructions; rather, it directs other parts of the system to do so. The control unit must communicate with both the arithmetic/logic unit and memory.

Discrete transistor and integrated circuit CPUs

The design complexity of CPUs increased as various technologies facilitated building smaller and more reliable electronic devices. The first such improvement came with the advent of the transistor. Transistorized CPUs during the 1950s and 1960s no longer had to be built out of bulky, unreliable, and fragile switching elements like vacuum tubes and electrical relays. With this improvement more complex and reliable CPUs were built onto one or several printed circuit boards containing discrete (individual) components.

CPU, core memory, and external bus interface of a DEC PDP-8/I. Made of medium-scale integrated circuits

During this period, a method of manufacturing many transistors in a compact space gained popularity. The integrated circuit (IC) allowed a large number of transistors to be manufactured on a single semiconductor-based die, or "chip." At first only very basic non-specialized digital circuits such as NOR gates were miniaturized into ICs. CPUs based upon these "building block" ICs are generally referred to as "small-scale integration" (SSI) devices. SSI ICs, such as the ones used in the Apollo guidance computer, usually contained up to a few score transistors. To build an entire CPU out of SSI ICs required thousands of individual chips, but still consumed much less space and power than earlier discrete transistor designs. As microelectronic technology advanced, an increasing number of transistors were placed on ICs, thus decreasing the quantity of individual ICs needed for a complete CPU. MSI and LSI (medium- and large-scale integration) ICs increased transistor counts to hundreds, and then thousands.

In 1964 IBM introduced its System/360 computer architecture which was used in a series of computers that could run the same programs with different speed and performance. This was significant at a time when most electronic computers were incompatible with one another, even those made by the same manufacturer. To facilitate this improvement, IBM utilized the concept of a microprogram (often called "microcode"), which still sees widespread usage in modern CPUs.[3] The System/360 architecture was so popular that it dominated the mainframe computer market for decades and left a legacy that is still continued by similar modern computers like the IBM zSeries. In the same year (1964), Digital Equipment Corporation (DEC) introduced another influential computer aimed at the scientific and research markets, the PDP-8. DEC would later introduce the extremely popular PDP-11 line that originally was built with SSI ICs but was eventually implemented with LSI components once these became practical. In stark contrast with its SSI and MSI predecessors, the first LSI implementation of the PDP-11 contained a CPU composed of only four LSI integrated circuits.[4]

Transistor-based computers had several distinct advantages over their predecessors. Aside from facilitating increased reliability and lower power consumption, transistors also allowed CPUs to operate at much higher speeds because of the short switching time of a transistor in comparison to a tube or relay. Thanks to both the increased reliability as well as the dramatically increased speed of the switching elements (which were almost exclusively transistors by this time), CPU clock rates in the tens of megahertz were obtained during this period. Additionally while discrete transistor and IC CPUs were in heavy usage, new high-performance designs like SIMD (Single Instruction Multiple Data) vector processors began to appear. These early experimental designs later gave rise to the era of specialized supercomputers like those made by Cray Inc.

Microprocessors

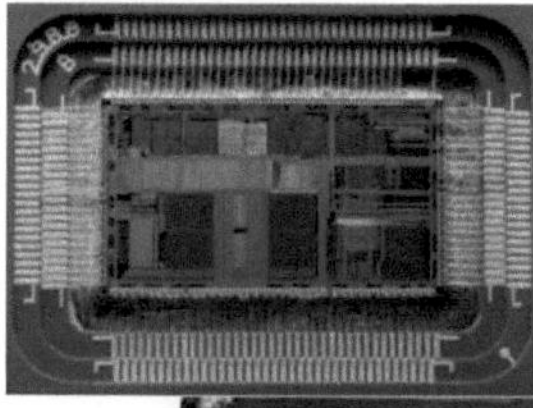

- Die of an Intel 80486DX2 microprocessor (actual size: 12×6.75 mm) in its packaging

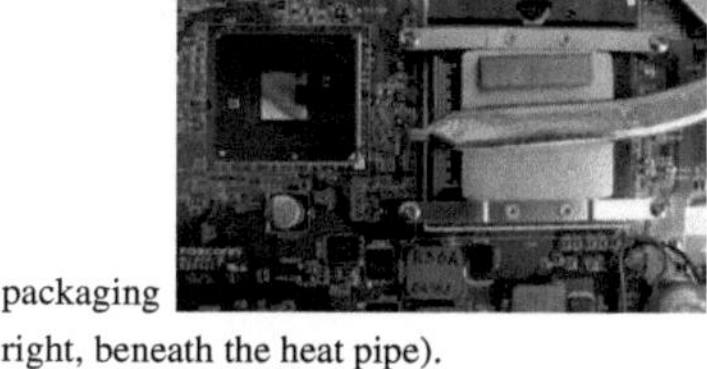

- Intel Core i5 CPU on a Vaio E series laptop motherboard (on the right, beneath the heat pipe).

In the 1970s the fundamental inventions by Federico Faggin (Silicon Gate MOS ICs with self aligned gates along with his new random logic design methodology) changed the design and implementation of CPUs forever. Since the introduction of the first commercially available microprocessor (the Intel 4004) in 1970, and the first widely used microprocessor (the Intel 8080) in 1974, this class of CPUs has almost completely overtaken all other central processing unit implementation methods. Mainframe and minicomputer manufacturers of the time launched proprietary IC development programs to upgrade their older computer architectures, and eventually produced instruction set compatible microprocessors that were backward-compatible with their older hardware and software. Combined with the advent and eventual vast success of the now ubiquitous personal computer, the term *CPU* is now applied almost exclusively to microprocessors. Several CPUs can be combined in a single processing chip.

Previous generations of CPUs were implemented as discrete components and numerous small integrated circuits (ICs) on one or more circuit boards. Microprocessors, on the other hand, are CPUs manufactured on a very small number of ICs; usually just one. The overall smaller CPU size as a result of being implemented on a single die means faster switching time because of physical factors like decreased gate parasitic capacitance. This has allowed synchronous microprocessors to have clock rates ranging from tens of megahertz to several gigahertz. Additionally, as the ability to construct exceedingly small transistors on an IC has increased, the complexity and number of transistors in a single CPU has increased dramatically. This widely observed trend is described by Moore's law, which has proven to be a fairly accurate predictor of the growth of CPU (and other IC) complexity to date.

While the complexity, size, construction, and general form of CPUs have changed drastically over the past sixty years, it is notable that the basic design and function has not changed much at all. Almost all common CPUs today can be very accurately described as von Neumann stored-program machines. As the aforementioned Moore's law continues to hold true, concerns have arisen about the limits of integrated circuit transistor technology. Extreme miniaturization of electronic gates is causing the effects of phenomena like electromigration and subthreshold leakage to become much more significant. These newer concerns are among the many factors causing researchers to investigate new methods of computing such as the quantum computer, as well as to expand the usage of parallelism and other methods that extend the usefulness of the classical von Neumann model.

Operation

The fundamental operation of most CPUs, regardless of the physical form they take, is to execute a sequence of stored instructions called a program. The program is represented by a series of numbers that are kept in some kind of computer memory. There are four steps that nearly all CPUs use in their operation: fetch, decode, execute, and writeback.

The first step, fetch, involves retrieving an instruction (which is represented by a number or sequence of numbers) from program memory. The location in program memory is determined by a program counter (PC), which stores a number that identifies the current position in the program. After an instruction is fetched, the PC is incremented by the length of the instruction word in terms of memory units.[5] Often, the instruction to be fetched must be retrieved from relatively slow memory, causing the CPU to stall while waiting for the instruction to be returned. This issue is largely addressed in modern processors by caches and pipeline architectures (see below).

The instruction that the CPU fetches from memory is used to determine what the CPU is to do. In the decode step, the instruction is broken up into parts that have significance to other portions of the CPU. The way in which the numerical instruction value is interpreted is defined by the CPU's instruction set architecture (ISA).[6] Often, one group of numbers in the instruction, called the opcode, indicates which operation to perform. The remaining parts of the number usually provide information required for that instruction, such as operands for an addition operation. Such operands may be given as a constant value (called an immediate value), or as a place to locate a value: a register or a memory address, as determined by some addressing mode. In older designs the portions of the CPU responsible for instruction decoding were unchangeable hardware devices. However, in more abstract and complicated CPUs and ISAs, a microprogram is often used to assist in translating instructions into various configuration signals for the CPU. This microprogram is sometimes rewritable so that it can be modified to change the way the CPU decodes instructions even after it has been manufactured.

After the fetch and decode steps, the execute step is performed. During this step, various portions of the CPU are connected so they can perform the desired operation. If, for instance, an addition operation was requested, the arithmetic logic unit (ALU) will be connected to a set of inputs and a set of outputs. The inputs provide the numbers to be added, and the outputs will contain the final sum. The ALU contains the circuitry to perform simple arithmetic and logical operations on the inputs (like addition and bitwise operations). If the addition operation produces a result too large for the CPU to handle, an arithmetic overflow flag in a flags register may also be set.

The final step, writeback, simply "writes back" the results of the execute step to some form of memory. Very often the results are written to some internal CPU register for quick access by subsequent instructions. In other cases results may be written to slower, but cheaper and larger, main memory. Some types of instructions manipulate the program counter rather than directly produce result data. These are generally called "jumps" and facilitate behavior like loops, conditional program execution (through the use of a conditional jump), and functions in programs.[7] Many instructions will also change the state of digits in a "flags" register. These flags can be used to influence how a program behaves, since they often indicate the outcome of various operations. For example, one type of "compare" instruction considers two values and sets a number in the flags register according to which one is greater. This flag could then be used by a later jump instruction to determine program flow.

After the execution of the instruction and writeback of the resulting data, the entire process repeats, with the next instruction cycle normally fetching the next-in-sequence instruction because of the incremented value in the program counter. If the completed instruction was a jump, the program counter will be modified to contain the address of the instruction that was jumped to, and program execution continues normally. In more complex CPUs than the one described here, multiple instructions can be fetched, decoded, and executed simultaneously. This section describes what is generally referred to as the "classic RISC pipeline", which in fact is quite common among the simple CPUs used in many electronic devices (often called microcontroller). It largely ignores the important role of CPU cache, and therefore the access stage of the pipeline.

Design and implementation

The basic concept of a CPU is as follows:

Hardwired into a CPU's design is a list of basic operations it can perform, called an instruction set. Such operations may include adding or subtracting two numbers, comparing numbers, or jumping to a different part of a program. Each of these basic operations is represented by a particular sequence of bits; this sequence is called the opcode for that particular operation. Sending a particular opcode to a CPU will cause it to perform the operation represented by that opcode. To execute an instruction in a computer program, the CPU uses the opcode for that instruction as well as its arguments (for instance the two numbers to be added, in the case of an addition operation). A computer program is therefore a sequence of instructions, with each instruction including an opcode and that operation's arguments.

The actual mathematical operation for each instruction is performed by a subunit of the CPU known as the arithmetic logic unit or ALU. In addition to using its ALU to perform operations, a CPU is also responsible for reading the next instruction from memory, reading data specified in arguments from memory, and writing results to memory.

In many CPU designs, an instruction set will clearly differentiate between operations that load data from memory, and those that perform math. In this case the data loaded from memory is stored in registers, and a mathematical operation takes no arguments but simply performs the math on the data in the registers and writes it to a new register, whose value a separate operation may then write to memory.

Integer range

The way a CPU represents numbers is a design choice that affects the most basic ways in which the device functions. Some early digital computers used an electrical model of the common decimal (base ten) numeral system to represent numbers internally. A few other computers have used more exotic numeral systems like ternary (base three). Nearly all modern CPUs represent numbers in binary form, with each digit being represented by some two-valued physical quantity such as a "high" or "low" voltage.[8]

MOS 6502 microprocessor in a dual in-line package, an extremely popular 8-bit design

Related to number representation is the size and precision of numbers that a CPU can represent. In the case of a binary CPU, a *bit* refers to one significant place in the numbers a CPU deals with. The number of bits (or numeral places) a CPU uses to represent numbers is often called "word size", "bit width", "data path width", or "integer precision" when dealing with strictly integer numbers (as opposed to floating point). This number differs between architectures, and often within different parts of the very same CPU. For example, an 8-bit CPU deals with a range of numbers that can be represented by eight binary digits (each digit having two possible values), that is, 2^8 or 256 discrete numbers. In effect, integer size sets a hardware limit on the range of integers the software run by the CPU can utilize.[9]

Integer range can also affect the number of locations in memory the CPU can address (locate). For example, if a binary CPU uses 32 bits to represent a memory address, and each memory address represents one octet (8 bits), the maximum quantity of memory that CPU can address is 2^{32} octets, or 4 GiB. This is a very simple view of CPU address space, and many designs use more complex addressing methods like paging to locate more memory than their integer range would allow with a flat address space.

Higher levels of integer range require more structures to deal with the additional digits, and therefore more complexity, size, power usage, and general expense. It is not at all uncommon, therefore, to see 4- or 8-bit microcontrollers used in modern applications, even though CPUs with much higher range (such as 16, 32, 64, even 128-bit) are available. The simpler microcontrollers are usually cheaper, use less power, and therefore generate less heat, all of which can be major design considerations for electronic devices. However, in higher-end applications, the benefits afforded by the extra range (most often the additional address space) are more significant and often affect design choices. To gain some of the advantages afforded by both lower and higher bit lengths, many CPUs are designed with different bit widths for different portions of the device. For example, the IBM System/370 used a CPU that was primarily 32 bit, but it used 128-bit precision inside its floating point units to facilitate greater accuracy and range in floating point numbers.[3] Many later CPU designs use similar mixed bit width, especially when the processor is meant for general-purpose usage where a reasonable balance of integer and floating point capability is required.

Clock rate

The clock rate is the speed at which a microprocessor executes instructions. Every computer contains an internal clock that regulates the rate at which instructions are executed and synchronizes all the various computer components. The CPU requires a fixed number of clock ticks (or clock cycles) to execute each instruction. The faster the clock, the more instructions the CPU can execute per second.

Most CPUs, and indeed most sequential logic devices, are synchronous in nature.[10] That is, they are designed and operate on assumptions about a synchronization signal. This signal, known as a clock signal, usually takes the form of a periodic square wave. By calculating the maximum time that electrical signals can move in various branches of a CPU's many circuits, the designers can select an appropriate period for the clock signal.

This period must be longer than the amount of time it takes for a signal to move, or propagate, in the worst-case scenario. In setting the clock period to a value well above the worst-case propagation delay, it is possible to design the entire CPU and the way it moves data around the "edges" of the rising and falling clock signal. This has the advantage of simplifying the CPU significantly, both from a design perspective and a component-count perspective. However, it also carries the disadvantage that the entire CPU must wait on its slowest elements, even though some portions of it are much faster. This limitation has largely been compensated for by various methods of increasing CPU parallelism. (see below)

However, architectural improvements alone do not solve all of the drawbacks of globally synchronous CPUs. For example, a clock signal is subject to the delays of any other electrical signal. Higher clock rates in increasingly complex CPUs make it more difficult to keep the clock signal in phase (synchronized) throughout the entire unit. This has led many modern CPUs to require multiple identical clock signals to be provided to avoid delaying a single signal significantly enough to cause the CPU to malfunction. Another major issue as clock rates increase dramatically is the amount of heat that is dissipated by the CPU. The constantly changing clock causes many components to switch regardless of whether they are being used at that time. In general, a component that is switching uses more energy than an element in a static state. Therefore, as clock rate increases, so does heat dissipation, causing the CPU to require more effective cooling solutions.

One method of dealing with the switching of unneeded components is called clock gating, which involves turning off the clock signal to unneeded components (effectively disabling them). However, this is often regarded as difficult to implement and therefore does not see common usage outside of very low-power designs. One notable late CPU design that uses clock gating is that of the IBM PowerPC-based Xbox 360. It utilizes extensive clock gating to reduce the power requirements of the aforementioned videogame console in which it is used.[11] Another method of addressing some of the problems with a global clock signal is the removal of the clock signal altogether. While removing the global clock signal makes the design process considerably more complex in many ways, asynchronous (or clockless) designs carry marked advantages in power consumption and heat dissipation in comparison with similar synchronous designs. While somewhat uncommon, entire asynchronous CPUs have been built without utilizing a global clock signal. Two notable examples of this are the ARM compliant AMULET and the MIPS R3000 compatible MiniMIPS. Rather than totally removing the clock signal, some CPU designs allow certain portions of the device to be asynchronous, such as using asynchronous ALUs in conjunction with superscalar pipelining to achieve some arithmetic performance gains. While it is not altogether clear whether totally asynchronous designs can perform at a comparable or better level than their synchronous counterparts, it is evident that they do at least excel in simpler math operations. This, combined with their excellent power consumption and heat dissipation properties, makes them very suitable for embedded computers.[12]

Parallelism

The description of the basic operation of a CPU offered in the previous section describes the simplest form that a CPU can take. This type of CPU, usually referred to as *subscalar*, operates on and executes one instruction on one or two pieces of data at a time.

Model of a subscalar CPU. Notice that it takes fifteen cycles to complete three instructions.

This process gives rise to an inherent inefficiency in subscalar CPUs. Since only one instruction is executed at a time, the entire CPU must wait for that instruction to complete before proceeding to the next instruction. As a result, the subscalar CPU gets "hung up" on instructions which take more than one clock cycle to complete execution. Even adding a second execution unit (see below) does not improve performance much; rather than one pathway being hung up, now two pathways are hung up and the number of unused transistors is increased. This design, wherein the CPU's execution resources can operate on only one instruction at a time, can only possibly reach *scalar* performance (one instruction per clock). However, the performance is nearly always subscalar (less than one instruction per cycle).

Attempts to achieve scalar and better performance have resulted in a variety of design methodologies that cause the CPU to behave less linearly and more in parallel. When referring to parallelism in CPUs, two terms are generally used to classify these design techniques. Instruction level parallelism (ILP) seeks to increase the rate at which instructions are executed within a CPU (that is, to increase the utilization of on-die execution resources), and thread level parallelism (TLP) purposes to increase the number of threads (effectively individual programs) that a CPU can execute simultaneously. Each methodology differs both in the ways in which they are implemented, as well as the relative effectiveness they afford in increasing the CPU's performance for an application.[13]

Instruction level parallelism

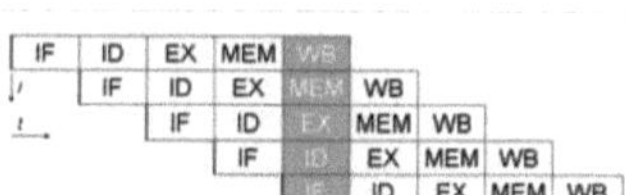
Basic five-stage pipeline. In the best case scenario, this pipeline can sustain a completion rate of one instruction per cycle.

One of the simplest methods used to accomplish increased parallelism is to begin the first steps of instruction fetching and decoding before the prior instruction finishes executing. This is the simplest form of a technique known as instruction pipelining, and is utilized in almost all modern general-purpose CPUs. Pipelining allows more than one instruction to be executed at any given time by breaking down the execution pathway into discrete stages. This separation can be compared to an assembly line, in which an instruction is made more complete at each stage until it exits the execution pipeline and is retired.

Pipelining does, however, introduce the possibility for a situation where the result of the previous operation is needed to complete the next operation; a condition often termed data dependency conflict. To cope with this, additional care must be taken to check for these sorts of conditions and delay a portion of the instruction pipeline if this occurs. Naturally, accomplishing this requires additional circuitry, so pipelined processors are more complex than subscalar ones (though not very significantly so). A pipelined processor can become very nearly scalar, inhibited only by pipeline stalls (an instruction spending more than one clock cycle in a stage).

Further improvement upon the idea of instruction pipelining led to the development of a method that decreases the idle time of CPU components even further. Designs that are said to be *superscalar* include a long instruction pipeline and multiple identical execution units.[14] In a superscalar pipeline, multiple instructions are read and passed to a dispatcher, which decides whether or not the instructions can be executed in parallel (simultaneously). If so they are dispatched to available execution units, resulting in the ability for several instructions to be executed simultaneously. In general, the more instructions a superscalar CPU is able to dispatch simultaneously to waiting execution units, the more instructions will be completed in a given cycle.

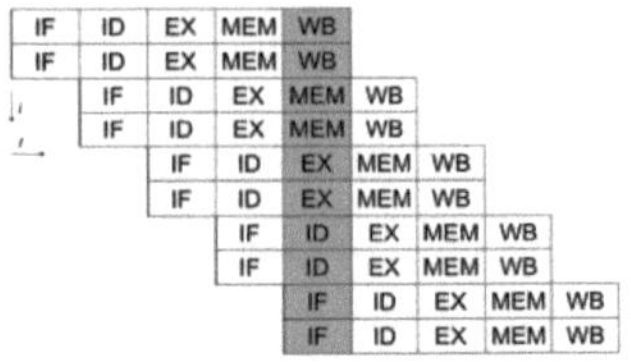

IF	ID	EX	MEM	WB
IF	ID	EX	MEM	WB

Simple superscalar pipeline. By fetching and dispatching two instructions at a time, a maximum of two instructions per cycle can be completed.

Most of the difficulty in the design of a superscalar CPU architecture lies in creating an effective dispatcher. The dispatcher needs to be able to quickly and correctly determine whether instructions can be executed in parallel, as well as dispatch them in such a way as to keep as many execution units busy as possible. This requires that the instruction pipeline is filled as often as possible and gives rise to the need in superscalar architectures for significant amounts of CPU cache. It also makes hazard-avoiding techniques like branch prediction, speculative execution, and out-of-order execution crucial to maintaining high levels of performance. By attempting to predict which branch (or path) a conditional instruction will take, the CPU can minimize the number of times that the entire pipeline must wait until a conditional instruction is completed. Speculative execution often provides modest performance increases by executing portions of code that may not be needed after a conditional operation completes. Out-of-order execution somewhat rearranges the order in which instructions are executed to reduce delays due to data dependencies. Also in case of Single Instructions Multiple Data — a case when a lot of data from the same type has to be processed, modern processors can disable parts of the pipeline so that when a single instruction is executed many times, the CPU skips the fetch and decode phases and thus greatly increases performance on certain occasions, especially in highly monotonous program engines such as video creation software and photo processing.

In the case where a portion of the CPU is superscalar and part is not, the part which is not suffers a performance penalty due to scheduling stalls. The Intel P5 Pentium had two superscalar ALUs which could accept one instruction per clock each, but its FPU could not accept one instruction per clock. Thus the P5 was integer superscalar but not floating point superscalar. Intel's successor to the P5 architecture, P6, added superscalar capabilities to its floating point features, and therefore afforded a significant increase in floating point instruction performance.

Both simple pipelining and superscalar design increase a CPU's ILP by allowing a single processor to complete execution of instructions at rates surpassing one instruction per cycle (IPC).[15] Most modern CPU designs are at least somewhat superscalar, and nearly all general purpose CPUs designed in the last decade are superscalar. In later years some of the emphasis in designing high-ILP computers has been moved out of the CPU's hardware and into its software interface, or ISA. The strategy of the very long instruction word (VLIW) causes some ILP to become implied directly by the software, reducing the amount of work the CPU must perform to boost ILP and thereby reducing the design's complexity.

Thread-level parallelism

Another strategy of achieving performance is to execute multiple programs or threads in parallel. This area of research is known as parallel computing. In Flynn's taxonomy, this strategy is known as Multiple Instructions-Multiple Data or MIMD.

One technology used for this purpose was multiprocessing (MP). The initial flavor of this technology is known as symmetric multiprocessing (SMP), where a small number of CPUs share a coherent view of their memory system. In this scheme, each CPU has additional hardware to maintain a constantly up-to-date view of memory. By avoiding stale views of memory, the CPUs can cooperate on the same program and programs can migrate from one CPU to another. To increase the number of cooperating CPUs beyond a handful, schemes such as non-uniform memory access (NUMA) and directory-based coherence protocols were introduced in the 1990s. SMP systems are limited to a small number of CPUs while NUMA systems have been built with thousands of processors. Initially, multiprocessing was built using multiple discrete CPUs and boards to implement the interconnect between the processors. When the processors and their interconnect are all implemented on a single silicon chip, the technology is known as a multi-core microprocessor.

It was later recognized that finer-grain parallelism existed with a single program. A single program might have several threads (or functions) that could be executed separately or in parallel. Some of the earliest examples of this technology implemented input/output processing such as direct memory access as a separate thread from the computation thread. A more general approach to this technology was introduced in the 1970s when systems were designed to run multiple computation threads in parallel. This technology is known as multi-threading (MT). This approach is considered more cost-effective than multiprocessing, as only a small number of components within a CPU is replicated to support MT as opposed to the entire CPU in the case of MP. In MT, the execution units and the memory system including the caches are shared among multiple threads. The downside of MT is that the hardware support for multithreading is more visible to software than that of MP and thus supervisor software like operating systems have to undergo larger changes to support MT. One type of MT that was implemented is known as block multithreading, where one thread is executed until it is stalled waiting for data to return from external memory. In this scheme, the CPU would then quickly switch to another thread which is ready to run, the switch often done in one CPU clock cycle, such as the UltraSPARC Technology. Another type of MT is known as simultaneous multithreading, where instructions of multiple threads are executed in parallel within one CPU clock cycle.

For several decades from the 1970s to early 2000s, the focus in designing high performance general purpose CPUs was largely on achieving high ILP through technologies such as pipelining, caches, superscalar execution, out-of-order execution, etc. This trend culminated in large, power-hungry CPUs such as the Intel Pentium 4. By the early 2000s, CPU designers were thwarted from achieving higher performance from ILP techniques due to the growing disparity between CPU operating frequencies and main memory operating frequencies as well as escalating CPU power dissipation owing to more esoteric ILP techniques.

CPU designers then borrowed ideas from commercial computing markets such as transaction processing, where the aggregate performance of multiple programs, also known as throughput computing, was more important than the performance of a single thread or program.

This reversal of emphasis is evidenced by the proliferation of dual and multiple core CMP (chip-level multiprocessing) designs and notably, Intel's newer designs resembling its less superscalar P6 architecture. Late designs in several processor families exhibit CMP, including the x86-64 Opteron and Athlon 64 X2, the SPARC UltraSPARC T1, IBM POWER4 and POWER5, as well as several video game console CPUs like the Xbox 360's triple-core PowerPC design, and the PS3's 7-core Cell microprocessor.

Data parallelism

A less common but increasingly important paradigm of CPUs (and indeed, computing in general) deals with data parallelism. The processors discussed earlier are all referred to as some type of scalar device.[16] As the name implies, vector processors deal with multiple pieces of data in the context of one instruction. This contrasts with scalar processors, which deal with one piece of data for every instruction. Using Flynn's taxonomy, these two schemes of dealing with data are generally referred to as SIMD (single instruction, multiple data) and SISD (single instruction, single data), respectively. The great utility in creating CPUs that deal with vectors of data lies in optimizing tasks that tend to require the same operation (for example, a sum or a dot product) to be performed on a large set of data. Some classic examples of these types of tasks are multimedia applications (images, video, and sound), as well as many types of scientific and engineering tasks. Whereas a scalar CPU must complete the entire process of fetching, decoding, and executing each instruction and value in a set of data, a vector CPU can perform a single operation on a comparatively large set of data with one instruction. Of course, this is only possible when the application tends to require many steps which apply one operation to a large set of data.

Most early vector CPUs, such as the Cray-1, were associated almost exclusively with scientific research and cryptography applications. However, as multimedia has largely shifted to digital media, the need for some form of SIMD in general-purpose CPUs has become significant. Shortly after inclusion of floating point execution units started to become commonplace in general-purpose processors, specifications for and implementations of SIMD execution units also began to appear for general-purpose CPUs. Some of these early SIMD specifications like HP's Multimedia Acceleration eXtensions (MAX) and Intel's MMX were integer-only. This proved to be a significant impediment for some software developers, since many of the applications that benefit from SIMD primarily deal with floating point numbers. Progressively, these early designs were refined and remade into some of the common, modern SIMD specifications, which are usually associated with one ISA. Some notable modern examples are Intel's SSE and the PowerPC-related AltiVec (also known as VMX).[17]

Performance

The *performance* or *speed* of a processor depends on the clock rate (generally given in multiples of hertz) and the instructions per clock (IPC), which together are the factors for the instructions per second (IPS) that the CPU can perform.[18] Many reported IPS values have represented "peak" execution rates on artificial instruction sequences with few branches, whereas realistic workloads consist of a mix of instructions and applications, some of which take longer to execute than others. The performance of the memory hierarchy also greatly affects processor performance, an issue barely considered in MIPS calculations. Because of these problems, various standardized tests, often called "benchmarks" for this purpose—such as SPECint -- have been developed to attempt to measure the real effective performance in commonly used applications.

Processing performance of computers is increased by using multi-core processors, which essentially is plugging two or more individual processors (called *cores* in this sense) into one integrated circuit.[19] Ideally, a dual core processor would be nearly twice as powerful as a single core processor. In practice, however, the performance gain is far less, only about 50%,[19] due to imperfect software algorithms and implementation. Increasing the number of cores in a processor (i.e. dual-core, quad-core, etc.) increases the workload that a computer can handle. This means that the processor can now handle numerous asynchronous events, Interrupts, etc. which can take a toll on the CPU (Central Processing Unit) when overwhelmed. It is best to think of these numerous cores as different floors in a processing plant, with each floor handling a different task. Sometimes, these cores will handle the same tasks as cores adjacent to them if a single core is not enough to handle the information to prevent a crash.

Integrated heat spreader

IHS is usually made of copper covered with a nickel plating.

See also

- Accelerated Processing Unit
- Addressing mode
- CISC
- Computer bus
- Computer engineering
- CPU cooling
- CPU core voltage
- CPU design
- CPU power dissipation
- CPU socket
- Digital signal processor
- Execution unit
- Instruction pipeline
- List of CPU architectures
- Ring (computer security)
- RISC
- Stream processing
- True Performance Index
- Wait state

Notes

[1] Weik, Martin H. (1961). *A Third Survey of Domestic Electronic Digital Computing Systems* (http://ed-thelen.org/comp-hist/BRL61.html). Ballistic Research Laboratories. .

[2] *First Draft of a Report on the EDVAC* (http://www.virtualtravelog.net/entries/2003-08-TheFirstDraft.pdf). Moore School of Electrical Engineering, University of Pennsylvania. 1945. .

[3] Amdahl, G. M., Blaauw, G. A., & Brooks, F. P. Jr. (1964). *Architecture of the IBM System/360* (http://www.research.ibm.com/journal/rd/441/amdahl.pdf). IBM Research. .

[4] Digital Equipment Corporation (November 1975). "LSI-11 Module Descriptions" (http://www.classiccmp.org/bitsavers/pdf/dec/pdp11/1103/EK-LSI11-TM-002.pdf). *LSI-11, PDP-11/03 user's manual* (2nd ed.). Maynard, Massachusetts: Digital Equipment Corporation. pp. 4–3. .

[5] Since the program counter counts *memory addresses* and not *instructions,* it is incremented by the number of memory units that the instruction word contains. In the case of simple fixed-length instruction word ISAs, this is always the same number. For example, a fixed-length 32-bit instruction word ISA that uses 8-bit memory words would always increment the PC by 4 (except in the case of jumps). ISAs that use variable length instruction words,increment the PC by the number of memory words corresponding to the last instruction's length.

[6] Because the instruction set architecture of a CPU is fundamental to its interface and usage, it is often used as a classification of the "type" of CPU. For example, a "PowerPC CPU" uses some variant of the PowerPC ISA. A system can execute a different ISA by running an emulator.

[7] Some early computers like the Harvard Mark I did not support any kind of "jump" instruction, effectively limiting the complexity of the programs they could run. It is largely for this reason that these computers are often not considered to contain a CPU proper, despite their close similarity as stored program computers.

[8] The physical concept of voltage is an analog one by its nature, practically having an infinite range of possible values. For the purpose of physical representation of binary numbers, set ranges of voltages are defined as one or zero. These ranges are usually influenced by the circuit designs and operational parameters of the switching elements used to create the CPU, such as a transistor's threshold level.

[9] While a CPU's integer size sets a limit on integer ranges, this can (and often is) overcome using a combination of software and hardware techniques. By using additional memory, software can represent integers many magnitudes larger than the CPU can. Sometimes the CPU's ISA will even facilitate operations on integers larger than it can natively represent by providing instructions to make large integer arithmetic relatively quick. While this method of dealing with large integers is somewhat slower than utilizing a CPU with higher integer size, it is a

reasonable trade-off in cases where natively supporting the full integer range needed would be cost-prohibitive. See Arbitrary-precision arithmetic for more details on purely software-supported arbitrary-sized integers.

[10] In fact, all synchronous CPUs use a combination of sequential logic and combinational logic. (See boolean logic)

[11] Brown, Jeffery (2005). "Application-customized CPU design" (http://www-128.ibm.com/developerworks/power/library/pa-fpfxbox/ ?ca=dgr-lnxw07XBoxDesign). IBM developerWorks. . Retrieved 2005-12-17.

[12] Garside, J. D., Furber, S. B., & Chung, S-H (1999). *AMULET3 Revealed* (http://www.cs.manchester.ac.uk/apt/publications/papers/ async99_A3.php). University of Manchester Computer Science Department. .

[13] Neither ILP nor TLP is inherently superior over the other; they are simply different means by which to increase CPU parallelism. As such, they both have advantages and disadvantages, which are often determined by the type of software that the processor is intended to run. High-TLP CPUs are often used in applications that lend themselves well to being split up into numerous smaller applications, so-called "embarrassingly parallel problems". Frequently, a computational problem that can be solved quickly with high TLP design strategies like SMP take significantly more time on high ILP devices like superscalar CPUs, and vice versa.

[14] Huynh, Jack (2003). "The AMD Athlon XP Processor with 512KB L2 Cache" (http://courses.ece.uiuc.edu/ece512/Papers/Athlon.pdf). University of Illinois — Urbana-Champaign. pp. 6–11. . Retrieved 2007-10-06.

[15] Best-case scenario (or peak) IPC rates in very superscalar architectures are difficult to maintain since it is impossible to keep the instruction pipeline filled all the time. Therefore, in highly superscalar CPUs, average sustained IPC is often discussed rather than peak IPC.

[16] Earlier the term scalar was used to compare the IPC (instructions per cycle) count afforded by various ILP methods. Here the term is used in the strictly mathematical sense to contrast with vectors. See scalar (mathematics) and Vector (geometric).

[17] Although SSE/SSE2/SSE3 have superseded MMX in Intel's general purpose CPUs, later IA-32 designs still support MMX. This is usually accomplished by providing most of the MMX functionality with the same hardware that supports the much more expansive SSE instruction sets.

[18] "CPU Frequency" (http://www.cpu-world.com/Glossary/C/CPU_Frequency.html). *CPU World Glossary*. CPU World. 25 March 2008. . Retrieved 1 January 2010.

[19] "What is (a) multi-core processor?" (http://searchdatacenter.techtarget.com/sDefinition/0,,sid80_gci1015740,00.html). *Data Center Definitions*. SearchDataCenter.com. 27 March 2007. . Retrieved 1 January 2010.

References

- Hennessy, John A.; Goldberg, David (1996). *Computer Architecture: A Quantitative Approach*. Morgan Kaufmann Publishers. ISBN 1-55860-329-8.
- [a] Gary D. Knott (1974) *A proposal for certain process management and intercommunication primitives* (http:// doi.acm.org/10.1145/775280.775282) ACM SIGOPS Operating Systems Review. Volume 8, Issue 4 (October 1974). pp. 7 − 44
- [a] MIPS Technologies, Inc. (2005). *MIPS32 Architecture For Programmers Volume II: The MIPS32 Instruction Set* (http://www.mips.com/content/Documentation/MIPSDocumentation/ProcessorArchitecture/doclibrary). MIPS Technologies, Inc..
- [a] Smotherman, Mark (2005). "History of Multithreading" (http://www.cs.clemson.edu/~mark/multithreading. html). Retrieved 2005-12-19.

External links

Microprocessor designers

- Advanced Micro Devices (http://www.amd.com/) - Advanced Micro Devices, a designer of primarily x86-compatible personal computer CPUs.
- ARM Ltd (http://www.arm.com/) - ARM Ltd, one of the few CPU designers that profits solely by licensing their designs rather than manufacturing them. ARM architecture microprocessors are among the most popular in the world for embedded applications.
- Freescale Semiconductor (http://www.freescale.com/) (formerly of Motorola) - Freescale Semiconductor, designer of several embedded and SoC PowerPC based processors.
- IBM Microelectronics (http://www-03.ibm.com/chips/) - Microelectronics division of IBM, which is responsible for many POWER and PowerPC based designs, including many of the CPUs utilized in late video game consoles.

- Intel Corp (http://www.intel.com/) - Intel, a maker of several notable CPU lines, including IA-32 and IA-64. Also a producer of various peripheral chips for use with their CPUs.
- Microchip Technology Inc. (http://www.microchip.com/) - Microchip, developers of the 8 and 16-bit short pipleine RISC and DSP microcontrollers.
- MIPS Technologies (http://www.mips.com/) - MIPS Technologies, developers of the MIPS architecture, a pioneer in RISC designs.
- NEC Electronics (http://www.am.necel.com/) - NEC Electronics (http://www.am.necel.com/), developers of the 78K0 8-bit Architecture (http://www.am.necel.com/micro/product/all_8_general.html/), 78K0R 16-bit Architecture (http://www.am.necel.com/micro/product/all_16_general.html/), and V850 32-bit Architecture (http://www.am.necel.com/micro/product/all_32_general.html/).
- Sun Microsystems (http://www.sun.com/) - Sun Microsystems, developers of the SPARC architecture, a RISC design.
- Texas Instruments (http://www.ti.com/home_p_allsc) - Texas Instruments semiconductor division. Designs and manufactures several types of low-power microcontrollers among their many other semiconductor products.
- Transmeta (http://www.transmeta.com/) - Transmeta Corporation. Creators of low-power x86 compatibles like Crusoe and Efficeon.
- VIA Technologies (http://www.viatech.com/) - Taiwanese maker of low-power x86-compatible CPUs.

Further reading

- How Microprocessors Work (http://www.howstuffworks.com/microprocessor.htm) at HowStuffWorks
- 25 Microchips that shook the world (http://spectrum.ieee.org/25chips) - an article by the Institute of Electrical and Electronics Engineers

Supercomputing_in_Japan

Japan operates a number of centers for **supercomputing** which hold world records in speed, with the K computer becoming the world's fastest in June 2011.[1] [2] [3]

The K computer's performance is impressive, according to professor Jack Dongarra who maintains the TOP500 list of supercomputers, and it surpasses its next 5 competitors combined.[1] The K computer costs US$10 million a year to operate.[1]

Previous records

Japan's entry into supercomputing started in the 1980s, and among others, the SX-3 supercomputer family was developed by NEC

The Earth Simulator in Yokohama was the world's fastest supercomputer in 2004, but 7 years later the K computer in Kobe became over 60 times faster.

Corporation and announced in April 1989.[4] The SX-3/44R became the fastest supercomputer in the world in 1990. Fujitsu's Numerical Wind Tunnel supercomputer gained the top spot in 1993.

The K computer's placement on the top spot is seven years after Japan held the title in 2004.[1] [2] The Earth Simulator supercomputer built by NEC at the Japan Agency for Marine-Earth Science and Technology (JAMSTEC) was the fastest in the world at that time with a peak of 131 TFlops, using proprietary vector processing chips. The K computer, on the other hand, uses over 60,000 commercial scalar SPARC64 VIIIfx processors housed in over 600 cabinets. The fact that K computer is over 60 times faster than the Earth Simulator, and that the Earth Simulator ranks as the 68th system in the world 7 years after holding the top spot demonstrates both the rapid increase in top performance in Japan and the widespread growth of supercomputing technology worldwide.

Supercomputing centers

Comparison (June 2011)[5]

Top speed (Tflops)	Country	Number of computers in TOP500
8162	Japan	26
2566	China	61
1759	United States	255
1050	France	25
826	Germany	30
350	Russia	12
316	South Korea	4
275	United Kingdom	27

The GSIC Center at the Tokyo Institute of Technology houses the Tsubame 2.0 supercomputer, which has a peak of 2,288 Tflops and in June 2011 ranked 5th in the world.[6] It was developed at the Tokyo Institute of Technology in collaboration with NEC and HP, and has 1,400 nodes using both HP Proliant and NVIDIA Tesla processors.[7]

The RIKEN MDGRAPE-3 for molecular dynamics simulations of proteins is a special purpose petascale supercomputer at the Advanced Center for Computing and Communication, RIKEN in Wako, Saitama, just outside Tokyo. It uses over 4,800 custom MDGRAPE-3 chips, as well as Intel Xeon processors.[8] However, given that it is a special purpose computer, it can not appear on the TOP500 list which requires Linpack benchmarking.

The next significant system is Japan Atomic Energy Agency's PRIMERGY BX900 Fujitsu supercomputer. It is significantly slower, reaching 200 TFlops and ranking as the 38th in the world in 2011.[9] [10]

Historically, the Gravity Pipe (GRAPE) system for astrophysics at the University of Tokyo was distinguished not by its top speed of 64 Tflops, but by its cost and energy efficiency, having won the Gordon Bell Prize in 1999, at about $7 per megaflops, using special purpose processing elements. [11]

DEGIMA is a highly cost and energy-efficient computer cluster at the Nagasaki Advanced Computing Center, Nagasaki University. It is used for hierarchical N-body simulations and has a peak performance of 111 TFLOPS with an energy efficiency of 1376 MFLOPS/watt. The overall cost of the hardware was approximately US$500,000.[12] [13]

The Computational Simulation Centre, International Fusion Energy Research Centre of the ITER Broader Approach[14] /Japan Atomic Energy Agency operates a 1.52-PFLOPS supercomputer (currently operating at 442 TFLOPS) in Rokkasho, Aomori. The system, called Helios (aka Roku-chan), consists of 4410 bullx B510 compute blades, and is used for fusion simulation projects.

The University of Tokyo's Information Technology Center in Kashiwa, Chiba began operations of a 1.13-PFLOPS supercomputer system (Oakleaf-FX) in April 2012. The system uses a Fujitsu PRIMEHPC FX10 configuration, a commercial version of the K supercomputer, composed of 4,800 computing nodes of SPARC64 IXfx processors connected via 6-dimensional mesh/torus interconnect.[15]

Grid computing

Starting in 2003, Japan used grid computing in the National Research Grid Initiative (NAREGI) project to develop high-performance, scalable grids over very high-speed networks as a future computational infrastructure for scientific and engineering research.[16]

See also

- Computer science
- Computing
- History of supercomputing
- Personal supercomputer
- Supercomputer architecture
- Supercomputing in China
- Supercomputing in Europe
- Supercomputing in India
- TOP500

References

[1] "Japanese supercomputer 'K' is world's fastest" (http://www.telegraph.co.uk/technology/news/8586655/ Japanese-supercomputer-K-is-worlds-fastest.html). The Telegraph. 20 June 2011. . Retrieved 20 June 2011.

[2] "Japanese 'K' Computer Is Ranked Most Powerful" (http://www.nytimes.com/2011/06/20/technology/20computer.html). *The New York Times*. 20 June 2011. . Retrieved 20 June 2011.

[3] "Supercomputer "K computer" Takes First Place in World" (http://www.fujitsu.com/global/news/pr/archives/month/2011/ 20110620-02.html). Fujitsu. . Retrieved 20 June 2011.

[4] *Computing methods in applied sciences and engineering* by R. Glowinski, A. Lichnewsky ISBN 0898712645 page 353-360

[5] "TOP500 List - June 2011" (http://top500.org/list/2011/06/100). TOP500. . Retrieved 2011-06-22.

[6] HPCWire May 2011 (http://www.hpcwire.com/hpcwire/2011-05-05/ tokyo_institute_of_technology_to_add_cula_library_to_tsubame_2_0.html)

[7] Hui Pan 'Research Initiatives with HP Servers', Gigabit/ATM Newsletter, December 2010, page 11

[8] Carey, Bjorn (2006), "Overachievers We Love - Faster", *Popular Science* 269 (6)

[9] TOP500 (http://www.top500.org/system/10564)

[10] TOP500 ranking (http://www1.top500.org/system/ranking/10564)

[11] J Makino, *Specialized Hardware for Supercomputing*, SciDAC Review, Issue 12 (Spring 2009), IOP. 2009

[12] The Green500 June 2011 (http://www.green500.org/lists/2011/06/top/list.php) Environmentally Responsible Supercomputing, The Green500 List

[13] *190 TFlops Astrophysical N-body Simulation on a Cluster of GPUs* by T. Hamada, T. et al in: High Performance Computing, Networking, Storage and Analysis (SC), 2010 International Conference, New Orleans, LA, 13-19 Nov. 2010, pages 1 - 9

[14] ITER Broader Approach (http://fusionforenergy.europa.eu/understandingfusion/broaderapproach.aspx)

[15] Information Technology Center, The University of Tokyo (2011-11-14). "Fujitsu's PRIMEHPC FX10 with 1.13 PFLOPS starts operation at the University of Tokyo in April 2012" (http://www.itc.u-tokyo.ac.jp/news/2011/20111114e.pdf) (PDF). . Retrieved 2012-02-05.

[16] S. Matsuokaet et al. (March 2005). "Japanese Computational Grid Research Project: NAREGI". *Proceedings of the IEEE* **93** (3): 522–533. doi:10.1109/JPROC.2004.842748.

External links

- GSIC Center, Tokyo Institute of Technology (http://www.gsic.titech.ac.jp/en)
- The GRAPE site at the University of Tokyo (http://www.astrogrape.org)

Article Sources and Contributors

DEGIMA_(computer_cluster) *Source*: http://en.wikipedia.org/w/index.php?title=DEGIMA_%28computer_cluster%29 *Contributors*: History2007, Krtek2125, Ottawahitech

Nagasaki_University *Source*: http://en.wikipedia.org/w/index.php?title=Nagasaki_University *Contributors*: DerBorg, Doraemonplus, Fg2, Hasec, Hussein.abkallo, Jllm06, LeDoyen68, Nihonjoe, Patrick Schwemmer, Timrollpickering, 1 anonymous edits

N-body simulation *Source*: http://en.wikipedia.org/w/index.php?title=N-body_simulation *Contributors*: Aernst81, Biezl, Cowbert, Dude1818, Edward, FunnyMan3595, GrEp, GregorB, IanOsgood, Joke137, Jptdrake, Lookhigh, Michael Hardy, Night Gyr, Olaf Davis, Pengo, PrinceGloria, Rjwilmsi, RockSolidCosmo, Scog, Signalhead, Smerity, Spartaz, Stou, Yosef1987, Zundark, 15 anonymous edits

DDR3_SDRAM *Source*: http://en.wikipedia.org/w/index.php?title=DDR3_SDRAM *Contributors*: ACookr, AOK30, Adhirk, Airplaneman, Ajs1984, Alansohn, Ali@gwc.org.uk, Allstarecho, Angrytoast, Arch dude, Areseepee, AySz88, Bender235, Benjamin albert, Bettymnz4, Binba, BlindWanderer, Bob A, Bobblewik, Boemanneke, Boing! said Zebedee, Bowmanjj, C. Foultz, Can't sleep, clown will eat me, Colin Douglas Howell, CombatWombat42, CommonsDelinker, Corvus cornix, Csigabi, D. Recorder, DVdm, Darin-0, Dave laird, DaveJB, Defender of torch, Denniss, Diablo-D3, Digital infinity, DivineLight, Djgandy, DocWatson42, Drjt87, Drmies, Dual Freq, ELCleanup, Edetic, Ee79, Epbr123, Eugene-elgato, FT2, Facts707, Fatsamsgrandslam, Feneeth of Borg, Fernvale, FerrousTigrus, Finell, Fiskars007, FlyingPenguins, Fnagaton, Frap, GOV, Gameking123, Gavin86, Gcprakashh, Geekosaurus, Gildos, Giseong, Gogo Dodo, GregorB, GreyCat, Guy Harris, HallucigeniaUK, Ham Pastrami, Harizotoh9, Hdante, Hellcat fighter, Henk.muller, Hugowolf, IT DoNT, Iggee85, Iiaiiappa, Immunize, Isilanes, Itinerant1, Jaakobou, JavierMC, Jeffq, Jesse Viviano, Joey-das-WBF, Jts888, JustinRossi, KDesk, Kar.ma, Karam.Anthony.K, Kigali1, Kyng, LOL, Laptcd, Leandrod, Lezitor, Llloic, Locos epraix, Locriani, Ltwizard, Luigiacruz, Maghnus, Majidjanvaljan, Makelelecba, Marky540, Martiniturbide, Master-andra, Materialscientist, Mboehn, Megahmad, Mike.lifeguard, MilerWhite, Mindmatrix, MrESaulved!, MureninC, NJA, Nigeldh, Nikpapag, Ninjagecko, Noahspurrier, Olin Coles, Optikos, Otus, P2501, Paranoidmage, Pboyd04, Pedz221, Pfhorapedia, Pgk1, Picomp314, PluniAlmoni, QTCaptain, Quelrod, Ravagewing, Reddevil0728, Reddyuday, Rich Farmbrough, Rjwilmsi, Satusguy, Saxbryn, Sergei, SeriousWorm, Shadowjams, Shandris, Snoofer, Srikeit, Sterremix, Steveprutz, Superchad, Tarikash, Tax24cat, Therealdp, Thinpig, Thue, Timl2k4, Tomaxer, Tratten, Treedee, Versus22, ViperSnake151, Voidxor, W.F.Galway, Warren314, WhosAsking, Wikiwill, Winston Chuen-Shih Yang, Z hosen, Zalgo, Zangoo, שחזורים, 450 anonymous edits

GeForce_200_Series *Source*: http://en.wikipedia.org/w/index.php?title=GeForce_200_Series *Contributors*: Aaron Schulz, Agni451, Airplaneman, Alan Liefting, Alpinwolf, Annoyed with fanboys, Araris, Ash Nekkron, Blakegripling ph, Cavalary, CommonsDelinker, Csendesmark, Cyclonius, DMacks, Dagwiki, Denoir, Docu, Download, Editor34451, Enviroboy, FEAR6655, Feudonym, FleetCommand, FstrthnU, GRevolution824, Goodone121, GregorB, GuitarFreak, Hammersoft, Hyins, IKiddo, Imperator3733, Jbigler, Jeffq, Joffeloff, Joshery420, Joy, Jpgoelz, Jzhang, Kape kron799, Kbdank71, L337hunter, Lacp69, Leszek Jańczuk, Lklundin, Ltwizard, MacintoshWriter, Mathias-S, Matthew Yeager, Mewtu, Mind my edits, Moonriddengirl, Motorheadx, MrOllie, Muuki, NeOak, Normandy, Nussi, Onorem, Orbitalorbital, Otrfan, Pauli133, Petri Krohn, Pizzahut2, Praetor alpha, RedHillian, Ronark, Rpvdk, Saebjorn, Schnarr, Semi-Lobster, Siavash1989, Skorp, SkyWalker, Skybon, Soruly, Standalones, Tomáš Slavotínek, Tsnor, UKER, Vacatalada, ViveCulture, Vmaldia, Vsuontam, WannabeAmatureHistorian, Wax2k, Wrightbus, Wujuanyu, Yakiv Gluck, Δ, 578 anonymous edits

Graphics_processing_unit *Source*: http://en.wikipedia.org/w/index.php?title=Graphics_processing_unit *Contributors*: -Majestic-, 4wajzkd02, 5900FX, =Josh.Harris, AFBorchert, ALoopingIcon, Aayush.nitb, Academic Challenger, Accessory, Ae-a, Aeons, Agehu, Akkida, Aleenf1, AlexKepler, Alf Boggis, Ali@gwc.org.uk, Alison, AlistairMcMillan, Anabus, Andres, AndriusG, Andy16666, Angelic Wraith, Arch dude, Arnero, Aughtandzero, Beland, Ben Ben, Berkut, Bevo74, Bigbluefish, Bitsmart, Bjorke, Braddodson, Braxtonw1, Can't sleep, clown will eat me, Canadianbob, CanisRufus, Chealer, ChrisfromHouston, Clark89, Cody-7, Cogiati, Colinstu, Crazyideas21, Cxk271, Cybercobra, D'Agosta, DARTH SIDIOUS 2, DJSupreme23, David Biddulph, David Eppstein, Dcirovic, Delirium of disorder, Des3dhj, Diculous, Disavian, Djayjp, DopefishJustin, Dpmuk, Drhex, Dymatic, E Wing, Earthere, Easwarno1, Eberhart, EconomistBR, Edward, Egil, Egomaniac, El Krem, Eleven even, Erud, Everyking, Evice, FAMAS, FearTec, Fiftyquid, Flex Flint, Frap, Furrykef, Gadfium, Galoubet, Garde, GateKeeper, Gbrose85, GeoffMacartney, Gillwill, Gioto, GlasGhost, Glitchrf, Gogo Dodo, GoldDragon, Gracefool, Gronky, Gzkn, Handheldpenguin, HarisM, Harumphy, Harvester, Haseo9999, HeroTsai, Heron, Hexmaster, Hitachi-Train, Holden15, Hu12, Imroy, Isnow, IvarTJ, J.delanoy, J04n, JDP90, JJC1138, Jafet, Jagged 85, JanEnEm, Jannex, Jappalang, Jarble, Jdevesa, JeGX, Jerome Charles Potts, Jesse Viviano, Jessemv, Jo7hs2, Joffeloff, Johan.Seland, John Bouhan, Jpvinall, Jrockley, Jsmaye, Jtbandes, Kaf, Kangaroopower, Karada, Kbdank71, Kelly Martin, Khalid hassani, Kjkolb, Kremerica, Largecrashman, Lazulilasher, Lee Cremeans, Lightmouse, Lights, LilHelpa, Locke411, Lockeownzj00, Lurker, M412k, MER-C, MFNickster, Macronyx, Mahjongg, Marasmusine, Markpapadakis, Martial75, Masterofwiki666, Math1337, Matt Britt, Mattdj, MaxDZ8, Mc6809e, Melter, Mentifisto, Michaelothomas, Mike92591, Mikkow, Mirror Vax, Mr. XYZ, MrRK, Murphykieran, Nakon, Nekura, Niceguyedc, Nikevich, Nitro912gr, Nixdorf, Noctibus, NonNobisSolum, Nopetro, Octahedron80, Optim, Osarius, Oxymoron83, P99am, Panscient, Paul Pogonyshev, Pavel Vozenilek, PavelSolin, Pgan002, Pharaoh of the Wizards, Phatom87, Phranq, Pi Guy 31415, Pinkadelica, Pixel8, Placi1982, Playwrite, Publicly Visible, QTCaptain, Quadell, Qviri, RBBrittain, Ravenperch, Rchandra, Renku, RicReis, Richi, Rilak, Romdanen, Ronhjones, RoyBoy, RubyQ, Ruw1090, Rzęsor, SCEhardt, SEG88, Sahrin, Salam32, Sango123, Scissorhands1203, Sciurinæ, Scott Paeth, Sdornan, Serketan, Serpent's Choice, Sg227, ShadowHntr, Shandris, Simoneau, Sjf, Skarkkai, SkyWalker, Socks 01, Socrates2008, Soumya92, Spiesr, Stargaming, Stoakron97, Stocbuster, Stormie, StuartBrady, Sugarbat, Suruena, Swaaye, TOR, Tandral, Taw, Tbird20d, Technobadger, Tempshill, The Thing That Should Not Be, Theonlyedge, Thue, Thumperward, Tigeron, Tijok, TimBentley, Tomy9510, Topbanana, Topeil, Toussaint, Tr-the-maniac, Trieste, Trilobite, Trusader, Twsl, UnfriendlyFire, Unyoyega, Utcursch, Vapourmile, Varuna, Veikk0.ma, Veinor, Veritysense, Vespristiano, Victorbabkov, Vidsi, Vincentfpgarcia, Virek, Vitkovskiy Roman, Viznut, Vuurmeester, Wayne Hardman, Wbm1058, Wernher, Wibbble, WikipedianMarlith, Willking1979, Winstonliang, Wknight94, Woohookitty, Xcentaur, Xowets, Yogi m, Yulu, Yyy, Zephalis, Zodon, 544 anonymous edits

Performance_per_watt *Source*: http://en.wikipedia.org/w/index.php?title=Performance_per_watt *Contributors*: A5b, Andreas Kaufmann, Benjaminchiang, Bkil, CXCV, Davidprior, FuzTheCat, Gyro Copter, Hu12, Itinerant1, Jafet, Joshuamarius, KathrynLybarger, MMuzammils, Mandarax, Mindmatrix, NapoliRoma, Physchim62, Plouin, R'n'B, Rebroad, Rjwilmsi, Smyth, Thorwald, Tinucherian, Vikingforties, Zodon, 20 anonymous edits

FLOPS *Source*: http://en.wikipedia.org/w/index.php?title=FLOPS *Contributors*: -Majestic-, 10014derek, 16@r, A111poker, A5b, ACSE, Aaronanodide, Agentbla, Ahoerstemeier, Aleph0, Alex Kuper, Alpinwolf, AlyM, Amadude, Analogue Kid, Ancheta Wis, Arrenlex, Artefact1981, Arthur a stevens, AscendedAnathema, Atemperman, Autopilot, Avnjay, B1atv, Bachrach44, Bardeep7, Beckboyanch, BenFrantzDale, Bender235, Benlisquare, Bobo192, Bogdangiusca, Borgx, Borisborf, Boxter1977, Brachiator, Bradml, Briaboru, BrokenSegue, BrownsRock10, Bryanlyon, Bsadowski1, Bubba73, Bulgrien, Buo, CS46, Calaka, Camerajohn, CanisRufus, CardinalDan, Chairman S., Charles Gaudette, China Dialogue News, Chowbok, Chris S, Clay Juicer, Cncxbox, Codehydro, Colonies Chris, Constantine, Craig Mayhew, Crasshopper, D-Notice, DEC42, Darin-0, Darkstar1st, David Shay, Decora, Deglr6328, Dekimasu, Demonkey36, Descender, Diablo65, Dicklyon, Dismas, Doctorfluffy, Donatus, Donfbreed, Doulos Christos, Drakcap, E Pluribus Anthony, E946, Eb.eric, Ed Poor, Ellmist, Elpuellodiablo, Elroch, Emorlock, EncMstr, Endymi0n, Epachamo, Epbr123, ExNihilo, FalconZero, FeiTeng1000, Feureau, FidelFair, Firien, Furrykef, FuzTheCat, GCarty, Gatoatigrado, Gene Nygaard, Ghettosam3000, Gimeee, Gjeremy, Gomallen, Googol30, Gortu, GregorB, Gunter, Haage42, Hairhorn, Henriok, Herbee, Highcount, Hyperdeath, Iamfscked, Ilted, ImMAW, Infofarmer, Inoculatedcities, Isilanes, Ixfd64, JPG-GR, Jaganath, Jake Nelson, Jarhed, Jaxl, Jaysbro, Jbaxter2007, Jdlambert, Jdm64, Jeff Carr, Jemecki, Jeremy Visser, JeremyA, Jerryobject, Jerryseinfeld, Jessemv, Jevansen, Jfmantis, Jjalexand, Joelon, Joffeloff, Johnnaylor, JorgePeixoto, Josh3580, KDesk, Karada, Keraunos, Ketiltrout, Kigali1, KittenKiller, Komap, Kyle, Kynereth, Laksono, LeeG, Leibnitz, Leithp, LiDaobing, Lightmouse, Littlealien182, Lmenthe, Lordvolton, Ltwizard, Luk, Lurker, Mad Mac, Mangojuice, Marc Lacoste, MarcoosPL, Mat cross, Matthew Kornya, Maxrangeley, Mazca, Mbutts, Meand, Melca, Mgblair, Michael Hardy, Mikaey, Mike1942f, MikeGogulski, Mini-Geek, Mipadi, Mishac, Montrealais, MovGP0, Mrdempsey, Msh210, Mtpaley, Mufbard, Muéro, Myscrnnm, Mário e Dário, Nachmore, Nehalem, Nick Number, Nickshanks, Nigholith, Nitecow, Nneonneo, Nwatson, Ohiostandard, Onissum, Pdcer, Philthecow, Pk3r72owns, Pmetzger, Poli, ProjectTux, Qiq, Quantumelfmage, Qwertyus, RJEvans, RTC, RainbowOfLight, Rasmus Faber, Raul654, Ravensfan5252, Rebroad, Reinderien, Reject, Requen, Rhoonkim, Rich Farmbrough, Rilak, Rjwilmsi, Roaming, Roarbakk, RobertG, RobertStar20, Robertvan1, Robina Fox, RoyBoy, Rrburke, Rudibs, Ryoohkies, Sachinwiki53, Sam Ellens, Sapeli, Sasuke Sarutobi, Schopenhauer, Scientus, Sdornan, SeanAmh, Seb35, SebastianHelm, Seraphimblade, Shawnc, Shawnhath, Sholtar, Simoneau, Slash, Snowolf, SolarElectricVehicle, Sollosonic, Sonicology, Spinach Monster, Stepa, Stevenj, Stevertigo, Stevestrange, Stikonas, Stroppolo, Supersword, SweatDiver, Symmetric Chaos, TWDorr, TeeEmCee, Tempodivalse, Teoryn, TerraFrost, Teveten, Thatoneguy, The Anome, The Anonymous One, TheBilly, TheGreatConspiracy, TheWickerMan, Theone00, Thumperward, Thunderbird2, Thunderbrand, Tide rolls, Titus III, Tom NM, Trevor Bekolay, Uncaer9, Urhixidur, Vendettax, Vicarious, VictorAnyakin, Voidphoenix, WAS 4.250, Wapcaplet, Wernher, Whitepaw, Whkoh, Winterspan, Wolfgang Kufner, Woohookitty, Ww.ellis, Xakepxakep, Yannledu, Yst, Zdude255, ZeroOne, Zginder, Zodon, Zojj, Zoonfafer, Zotel, Zouavman Le Zouave, Пётр Петров, 695 anonymous edits

Central_processing_unit *Source*: http://en.wikipedia.org/w/index.php?title=Central_processing_unit *Contributors*: .:Ajvol:., 04satvinderbi, 11james22, 132qwerty, 16@r, 4I7.4I7, 4twenty42o, 7265, ABF, Acdx, Aceofskies05, Acroterion, Adam.Amory.97, Adam1213, Adamwisky, AdjustShift, Ahoerstemeier, Ahpook, Aiken drum, Aitias, Akaka, Akjar13, Akuyume, Alansohn, Alex, AlphaPyro, Alphachimp, AlyM, Ambuj.Saxena, Ameliorate!, Anakata, AnakngAraw, Ancheta Wis, Anchit singla, Andre Engels, Andreas.Persson, AndrewWTaylor, Andy Dingley, Andypandy.UK, Angela, Angelic Wraith, Anna Lincoln, Ano onymis, Anonymous editor, Antandrus, Aphaia, Arakunem, Arcadie, Arch dude, ArchStanton69, Archer3, ArchonMagnus, Arman Cagle, Art LaPella, Arthena, Arunib, Ashawley, Ashish Gaikwad, Atlant, AuburnPilot, Avono, Avraham, Axl, AzaToth, BACbKA, BRUTE, Banes, Beastathon, Beland, Ben ben ben ben ben jerry, Ben-Zin, Benjaminjkim, Benscripps, Berkut, Bichito, Big Bird, Bighead01753, Bigtimepeace, BillyPreset, Bionik276, Bitolado, Blainster, Blanchardb, Blargarg, Bloodshedder, Bob121, Bobanater, Bobblewik, Bobet, Bobo192, Bonadea, Bongwarrior, Bookofjude, Booyabazooka, Bowmanjj, Brheed Zonabp84, Brion VIBBER, Bsadowski1, Buletproofbrit, Bwrs, CJLL Wright, CKsquid, CZmarlin, Cactus.man, Calmer Waters, Camomen3000, Camoxide, Can't sleep, clown will eat me, CanadianLinuxUser, CanisRufus, Capricorn42, Captain-tucker, CaptainVindaloo, Catfish Jim and the soapdish, Cedars, Cessator, Chasingsol, Chowbok, Chuck Smith, Chuq, Chuunen Baka, Cimon Avaro, Ck lostsword, Cogiati, Cohesion, Cometstyles, CommonsDelinker, Computerwoman417, Cpusweden, Crusadeonilliteracy, Ctjf83, Cuchullain, Cureden, Curps, Cybercobra, Cyrius, D0762, DARTH SIDIOUS 2, Damicatz, Dan Granahan, Dan100, Darklightning1, DarthShrine, Dauntless28, Dave314159, David Gerard, DavidCary, Davo123, Deelkar, Deerstop, Defender of torch, Deicool, Dekisugi, Demus Wiesbaden, DerHexer, Dhiraj1984, Diego UFCG, Dinshoupang, Discospinster, Dlohcierekim's sock, Dmsar, Dmytheus, Doczilla, Dogah, Dogan900, Don4of4, Donarreiskoffer, Dr.alf, DragonHawk, Druiloor, Duk, Dulciana, Dureo,

DwightKingsbury, Dyl, Ebricca, Edderso, Edonovan, Edward, Edwy, Ekilfeather, Ekonomka, Elano, Eleassar777, Electron20, Elfguy, Elipongo, Eliz81, Emperorbma, Emre D., Enviroboy, Epbr123, Epic matt, Erin2003, Espoo, Ettrig, Everyking, Evil saltine, Excirial, FMAlchemist36, Fabartus, Fallout boy, Fanf, Farosdaughter, Fastily, Fatal-, Feezo, Feinoha, Fieldday-sunday, Finell, Fir0002, Fiskars007, FleetCommand, Flewis, Flipper344, Fnagaton, Foxj, Frak, Frap, Freakofnurture, Frecklefoot, Fred Gandt, Fredrik, Frymaster, Fvasconcellos, Fæ, GB fan, Gail, Galoubet, Garion96, Genius1789, George The Dragon, GeorgeBills, Georgeb92, GermanX, Giftlite, Gilliam, Gimmetrow, Giraffedata, Glane23, Glenn, Gmb1994, Gogo Dodo, Gohst, Goodone121, GraemeL, Graham Jones, Graham87, Greg.Kerr01, GregorB, Gregory Shantz, Grungerz, Gseandiyh79, Guanaco, Gurch, Guy Harris, Gwandoya, Gwernol, Hadal, Hakufu Sonsaku, Hallo990, HandyAndy, Hans Dunkelberg, Harpastum, Haseo9999, Hashar, Hazal018, Headbangerbuggy, Heron, Hmains, Hmdz105, Hobartimus, Hotcrocodile, Htl848, Hydrogen Iodide, Iain.mcclatchie, Icelight, Ida Shaw, Ihateblazing, Ikiroid, Ilion2, Imdaking, Imperial Monarch, Info lover, Instigate cjsc (Narine), Instinct, Ipsign, IraChesterfield, Iridescent, Ironholds, Iwan rahabok, Ixfd64, J.delanoy, J128, JForget, JHMM13, Jab843, Jackfork, Jacoplane, Jacopone, James086, Jamesooders, Jan1nad, Jarred.rop1, Jasper Deng, Java13690, Jaxl, Jbray3179, Jcoy, Jd027, JeLuF, Jebus989, Jeff G., Jeffreyarcand, Jennavecia, Jeremy Visser, JesseW, JiFish, JinJian, Jiy, Jjtennisman, Jmabel, JoanneB, Joelr31, John Quincy Adding Machine, JohnFromPinckney, Johnteslade, JonHarder, Jonas weepel, Jondel, Jorgenev, Joyous!, Jpk, Jpkoester1, Jrstern29, Juhuang, Justinc, K1Bond007, Kabu, Karderio, Kbdank71, Keilana, Kelpherder, Kesac, Killdevil, King of Hearts, Kipala, Klaser, Knepflerle, Knockwood, Knowitall44, KnowledgeOfSelf, Koishii1521, Kozuch, Krawi, Krich, Ks0stm, Kubanczyk, Kudz75, Kuru, LHvU, LOL, LaMenta3, Landon1980, Lankiveil, Lanky217, LaughingMan42, Lauri.pirttiaho, LeaveSleaves, Lectonar, LeeDanielCrocker, Leon7, LevelCheck, Levineps, Lg1223, Liao, Liftarn, Lightmouse, Ligulem, Lilac Soul, Little Mountain 5, LittleOldMe, Littleog, Lmno, Longhair, LordJeff, Loren.wilton, Lou.weird, Luna Santin, Lupin, MC MasterChef, MECU, MONGO, Mac, Mahjongg, Malcolm, Malmis, Mandarax, Mandetory, Mani1, MansonP, Manta7, MantridFreeman, Manuel Trujillo Berges, Mapolat, MarSch, Marek69, Martin451, Materialscientist, Matey, Matt 118118, Matt Britt, Matthewirwin28693, Matticus78, Mav, Mayooranathan, Mbarbier, Mcdennis13, Mcicogni, Meiskam, Melsaran, Mentifisto, Merovingian, Michael Hardy, Microcell, Mikael Häggström, Mike Dill, Mike92591, Milf&cookies, Minesweeper, Minimac, Miranda, Misza13, Mitsuhirato, Mjbt, Mjpieters, Mmccalpin, Mmxx, Modulatum, Momma69, Monkeynoze, MooresLaw, Morkork, Mortense, Morwen, Mpgenius, MrOllie, Mudlock, Muriel Gottrop, Murray Langton, Mxn, Mygerardromance, Myhellhereorunder, Mynameiswa, MysticMetal, NPrice, Nagy, Nanshu, Nashhinton, NawlinWiki, Nayvik, Neelix, Neilc, NellieBly, Netanel h, Netoholic, NewEnglandYankee, Newton2, NickBush24, Nihiltres, Nikai, Nixdorf, Nixeagle, Noypi380, Nsaa, Nuggetboy, Nv8200p, Nxavar, Ohnoitsjamie, Oleg Alexandrov, Olie93, Omicronpersei8, Omiks3, Optakeover, Orange Suede Sofa, Orphan Wiki, Oxymoron83, P.B. Pilhet, PZFUN, Paolo.dL, Paul August, Pearcej, Pearle, Persian Poet Gal, Personline, Peruvianllama, Peti1212, Pgk, Phaldo, Phantomsteve, Pharaoh of the Wizards, Phatstakks, Pheeror, Phgao, Phil Boswell, Philip Trueman, Piano non troppo, Pilotguy, Pinkadelica, Pixel8, Pointillist, Pol098, Pololei, Pooosihole, Popup, Positron, Pranayrocks23, Priver312, Prodego, Pyfan, Qmwne235, Quadell, Quale, Quantyz, Qwyrxian, Qxz, R twell27, R'n'B, R. S. Shaw, RMartin-2, RTC, Radiopathy, Raghavkvp, Rajayush78, Ravenperch, RazorICE, Rdsmith4, Reach Out to the Truth, Reisio, Renamed user 1752, Res2216firestar, RexNL, Rhobite, Richi, Richwales, Rick Sidwell, Ridge Runner, RightSideNov, Rilak, RipFire12901, Rjclaudio, Robert K S, RobertG, Robost, Rome109, Ronhjones, Rowan Moore, Rprpr, Rror, Rsrikanth05, Ruud Koot, Rwwww, RyanParis, Rzęsor, S raghu20, SCARECROW, SEG88, SGBailey, ST47, SWAdair, Sahrin, Sam42, Sango123, Sasquatch, Savemeto2, Sax Russell, Sceptre, Scientus, Scriptfan, Sdfsakjdhfuioaheif283, Sean.hoyland, Seanm924, Seaphoto, Secretlondon, Sensiblemayank, Shadowjams, Shanes, Shawnc, Shell Kinney, Shizhao, Shoessss, Shrikanthv, Sicklight, SimonP, Sir Hat, Slavy13, Smurrayinchester, Snigbrook, Sniper-ass, Snowmanmelting, Snowolf, Soir, Solipsist, Solitude, Solphusion, Someguy1221, Sonicology, Sp, SpaceFlight89, Spacepotato, Specs112, Spike Wilbury, Spliffy, Srce, Starcraft.nut, Stas3717, Steel, Stephenb, SteveBaker, Stevertigo, Suruena, Sverdrup, Sychen, Synchrite, TakuyaMurata, Tarquin, Tawker, Taxman, Tbhotch, Techman224, Tempshill, Terence, TexasAndroid, The Anome, The High Fin Sperm Whale, The Ice Inside, The Thing That Should Not Be, The dragon123, The sock that should not be, TheJosh, TheKMan, Thesalus, Think outside the box, Thisisafakeaccountfordeletingpages, Tide rolls, Tigga en, Tim1980tim, Timir Saxa, Timl2k4, Timmy2, Tinton5, Tiptoety, ToastyMallows, Tom harrison, TomBridle, Tomeasy, Tommy Kronkvist, Tone, Tony1, TonySt, ToobMug, Tophtucker, Torahjerus14, Toussaint, Tpbradbury, Traroth, Tree Biting Conspiracy, Triggerhappy412, Trusilver, Tslocum, Ttwaring, Tuoreco, Turnerj, Tyler, Uncle Dick, Unixguy, Upholder, Useight, Uzume, VI, VampWillow, Velella, Versus22, Vikingstad, Vrenator, Vssun, Vulcanstar6, WJetChao, Wapcaplet, WardMuylaert, Wasted Sapience, Wavelength, Wayne Hardman, Wayne Slam, Wayward, Wbm1058, Wdfowty, Whispering, WhiteNebula, Who, Wiki alf, WikiDegausser, WikiLaurent, Wikiloop, WikipedianMarlith, Willtron, Wilson44691, Wimt, Windchaser, Winstonliang6758, Wiz126, Wizardist, Wjbeaty, Wouterstomp, Wtshymanski, Wx4sno, X360Silent, X5UPR3ME STEV3x, XJamRastafire, XTerminator2000, Xaosflux, Xenobog, Xoneca, Yabeeno, Yaronf, Yidisheryid, YourUserHere, Yucel114, Z.E.R.O., ZeWrestler, Zelphar, ZeroOne, Zidonuke, Zippedmartin, Zodon, Zzuuzz, fw-us-hou-8.bmc.com, Саша Стефановић, ‏ای ساروں ی‏, 1932 anonymous edits

Supercomputing_in_Japan *Source*: http://en.wikipedia.org/w/index.php?title=Supercomputing_in_Japan *Contributors*: Digidestiny, Edward321, Geniac, Giraffedata, History2007, KConWiki, Krtek2125, Northamerica1000, Piledhigheranddeeper, W Nowicki, Yomangani

Image Sources, Licenses and Contributors

File:Nagasaki Medical College.jpg *Source*: http://en.wikipedia.org/w/index.php?title=File:Nagasaki_Medical_College.jpg *License*: unknown *Contributors*:

File:Nagasaki 1945 - Before and after (adjusted).jpg *Source*: http://en.wikipedia.org/w/index.php?title=File:Nagasaki_1945_-_Before_and_after_(adjusted).jpg *License*: unknown *Contributors*: . U.S. National Archives : RG 77-MDH (according to William Burr, The Atomic Bomb and the End of World War II, National Security Archive Electronic Briefing Book No. 162).

File:NagasakiUniv Katafuchi KeirinHall.jpg *Source*: http://en.wikipedia.org/w/index.php?title=File:NagasakiUniv_Katafuchi_KeirinHall.jpg *License*: unknown *Contributors*: Original uploader was Jazzy at ja.wikipedia

File:AstroMSseqF 063aL (18135101).jpg *Source*: http://en.wikipedia.org/w/index.php?title=File:AstroMSseqF_063aL_(18135101).jpg *License*: unknown *Contributors*: Rich Murray from Santa Fe, New Mexico 87505, USA

File:4GB DDR3 SO-DIMM.jpg *Source*: http://en.wikipedia.org/w/index.php?title=File:4GB_DDR3_SO-DIMM.jpg *License*: unknown *Contributors*: User:Tobias b köhler

Image:Desktop DDR Memory Comparison.svg *Source*: http://en.wikipedia.org/w/index.php?title=File:Desktop_DDR_Memory_Comparison.svg *License*: unknown *Contributors*: User:Martini

Image:Laptop_SODIMM_DDR_Memory_Comparison_V2.svg *Source*: http://en.wikipedia.org/w/index.php?title=File:Laptop_SODIMM_DDR_Memory_Comparison_V2.svg *License*: unknown *Contributors*: Martini, Tothwolf

Image:GeForce newlogo.png *Source*: http://en.wikipedia.org/w/index.php?title=File:GeForce_newlogo.png *License*: unknown *Contributors*: Mr. XYZ, Rpvdk, SimGuy74

Image:6600GT GPU.jpg *Source*: http://en.wikipedia.org/w/index.php?title=File:6600GT_GPU.jpg *License*: unknown *Contributors*: User:Berkut

File:Dstealth32.jpg *Source*: http://en.wikipedia.org/w/index.php?title=File:Dstealth32.jpg *License*: unknown *Contributors*: Swaaye

File:DIAMONDSTEALTH3D2000-top.JPG *Source*: http://en.wikipedia.org/w/index.php?title=File:DIAMONDSTEALTH3D2000-top.JPG *License*: unknown *Contributors*: Swaaye

File:Voodoo3-2000AGP.jpg *Source*: http://en.wikipedia.org/w/index.php?title=File:Voodoo3-2000AGP.jpg *License*: unknown *Contributors*: Original uploader was Swaaye at en.wikipedia

Image:AMD HD5470 GPU.JPG *Source*: http://en.wikipedia.org/w/index.php?title=File:AMD_HD5470_GPU.JPG *License*: unknown *Contributors*: User:Ravenperch

Image:Intel 80486DX2 top.jpg *Source*: http://en.wikipedia.org/w/index.php?title=File:Intel_80486DX2_top.jpg *License*: unknown *Contributors*: Denniss, Solipsist, 1 anonymous edits

Image:Intel 80486DX2 bottom.jpg *Source*: http://en.wikipedia.org/w/index.php?title=File:Intel_80486DX2_bottom.jpg *License*: unknown *Contributors*: Denniss, Solipsist

Image:Edvac.jpg *Source*: http://en.wikipedia.org/w/index.php?title=File:Edvac.jpg *License*: unknown *Contributors*: ArnoldReinhold, Infrogmation, Medium69, Tothwolf

Image:PDP-8i cpu.jpg *Source*: http://en.wikipedia.org/w/index.php?title=File:PDP-8i_cpu.jpg *License*: unknown *Contributors*: Robert Krten

Image:80486dx2-large.jpg *Source*: http://en.wikipedia.org/w/index.php?title=File:80486dx2-large.jpg *License*: unknown *Contributors*: A23cd-s, Adambro, Admrboltz, Artnnerisa, CarolSpears, Denniss, Greudin, Julia W, Kozuch, Martin Kozák, Mattbuck, Rjd0060, Rocket000, 11 anonymous edits

Image:EBIntel Corei5.JPG *Source*: http://en.wikipedia.org/w/index.php?title=File:EBIntel_Corei5.JPG *License*: unknown *Contributors*: User:Ravenperch

Image:MOS 6502AD 4585 top.jpg *Source*: http://en.wikipedia.org/w/index.php?title=File:MOS_6502AD_4585_top.jpg *License*: unknown *Contributors*: EugeneZelenko, German, Idrougge, Morkork, Wdwd

Image:Nopipeline.png *Source*: http://en.wikipedia.org/w/index.php?title=File:Nopipeline.png *License*: unknown *Contributors*: User:Poil

Image:Fivestagespipeline.png *Source*: http://en.wikipedia.org/w/index.php?title=File:Fivestagespipeline.png *License*: unknown *Contributors*: User:Poil

Image:Superscalarpipeline.svg *Source*: http://en.wikipedia.org/w/index.php?title=File:Superscalarpipeline.svg *License*: unknown *Contributors*: User:Amit6, User:Poil

File:Earth simulator ES2.jpg *Source*: http://en.wikipedia.org/w/index.php?title=File:Earth_simulator_ES2.jpg *License*: unknown *Contributors*: GenGen ()

File:Flag of Japan.svg *Source*: http://en.wikipedia.org/w/index.php?title=File:Flag_of_Japan.svg *License*: unknown *Contributors*: Anomie

File:Flag of the People's Republic of China.svg *Source*: http://en.wikipedia.org/w/index.php?title=File:Flag_of_the_People's_Republic_of_China.svg *License*: unknown *Contributors*: User:Denelson83, User:SKopp, User:Shizhao, User:Zscout370

File:Flag of the United States.svg *Source*: http://en.wikipedia.org/w/index.php?title=File:Flag_of_the_United_States.svg *License*: unknown *Contributors*: Anomie

File:Flag of France.svg *Source*: http://en.wikipedia.org/w/index.php?title=File:Flag_of_France.svg *License*: unknown *Contributors*: Anomie

File:Flag of Germany.svg *Source*: http://en.wikipedia.org/w/index.php?title=File:Flag_of_Germany.svg *License*: unknown *Contributors*: Anomie

File:Flag of Russia.svg *Source*: http://en.wikipedia.org/w/index.php?title=File:Flag_of_Russia.svg *License*: unknown *Contributors*: Anomie

File:Flag of South Korea.svg *Source*: http://en.wikipedia.org/w/index.php?title=File:Flag_of_South_Korea.svg *License*: unknown *Contributors*: Various

File:Flag of the United Kingdom.svg *Source*: http://en.wikipedia.org/w/index.php?title=File:Flag_of_the_United_Kingdom.svg *License*: unknown *Contributors*: Anomie, Mifter

Printed by Books on Demand GmbH, Norderstedt / Germany